HÀNYǓ

FOR INTERMEDIATE STUDENTS

• PETER CHANG • ALYCE MACKERRAS • YU HSIU-CHING •

STUDENT'S BOOK

STAGE 1

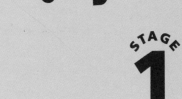

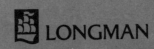

LONGMAN

Pearson Education Australia
A division of Pearson Australia Group Pty Ltd
Level 9, 5 Queens Road
Melbourne 3004 Australia

Offices in Sydney, Brisbane and Perth, and associated companies throughout the world.

Set in 10/11pt Helvetica (English and Pinyin) and
Simplified Kaisho (Chinese characters)
Produced by Pearson Education Australia
Printed in Malaysia, PJB

National Library of Australia
Cataloguing-in-Publication data

Chang, Peter
  Hànyǔ for intermediate students. Stage 1. Students book

  10 ISBN 0-582-80087-0. (Australia)
  13 ISBN 978-0-582-80087-8. (Australia)

  ISBN 0-88727-217-7 (USA)

  1. Chinese language - Textbooks for foreign speakers - English. 2.
  Chinese language - Problems, exercises, etc. 3. Chinese language -
  Writing. I. Mackerras, Alyce. II. Yu, Hsiu-ching. III. Title.

495.182421

Every effort has been made to trace and acknowledge copyright. However, should any
infringement have occurred, the publishers tender their apologies and invite copyright
owners to contact them.

Published with the support of the Key Centre for Asian Languages and Studies,
Griffith University programme.

Distributed in the United States and Canada by
Cheng and Tsui Company Inc.,
25 West Street
Boston MA02111-1268 USA

The
publisher's
policy is to use
**paper manufactured
from sustainable forests**

CONTENTS

ACKNOWLEDGEMENTS

The revision of the first volumes of the *Hànyǔ* series, of which *Hànyǔ for Intermediate Students Stage 1* represents the second stage, has been made possible by a grant from the Asian Studies Council and the authors would like to thank the Council for its support. We would also like to thank the Key Centre for Asian Languages and Studies, Faculty of Asian and International Studies, Griffith University and particularly its director, Professor Colin Mackerras, for the use of facilities and continued support for this project.

We would also like to thank the many teachers and students whose practical experience has contributed to the shape of the revisions. We would particularly like to thank Ms Chui Lee of The Southport School, Southport, who has been a principal consultant on the *Hànyǔ* course.

We especially wish to thank Ms Yin Guiqin and Professor Huang Zhengcheng of the Beijing Language Institute, who read the manuscript of *Hànyǔ for Intermediate Students Stage 1* and made many valuable comments.

We gratefully acknowledge the generosity of freelance photographer Mr Douglas Smith, who provided the photographs that appear on pages 4, 8, 57, 86, 116, 118, 124, 128, and 130.

INTRODUCTION

Recent decades have seen a growth in the study of Asian languages in Australia, reflecting the growing awareness of the importance of Asia in our cultural, economic and political life. The study of Chinese has been part of this growth, with Modern Standard Chinese being officially designated one of the 'languages of wider teaching', having significance to Australia for external and economic considerations as well as being an important community language within Australia itself.

The *Hànyǔ* series has been compiled in response to the need for Chinese language teaching materials suitable for Australian secondary students. The seeding funding for the series came from the Australia-China Council, which was set up by the Federal Government in 1979 to promote understanding between Australia and China. The first volume, *Hànyǔ 1*, was published in 1985, *Hànyǔ 2* was published in 1986 and *Hànyǔ 3* in 1990.

Hànyǔ for Intermediate Students Stage 1 represents the second stage in the revised editions of the first two volumes, *Hànyǔ 1* and *Hànyǔ 2*, of the *Hànyǔ* series. The revisions reflect the changing emphases in language teaching in Australia and are also a reponse to the practical needs of teachers and students in our schools. These revisions have been made possible by a grant from the Asian Studies Council.

The *Student's Book* is the basic volume for the *Hànyǔ for Intermediate Students Stage 1* course. It comprises four units, each designed around topics or general areas of communicative activity selected as ones that will enable students to use the Chinese language communicatively in their immediate environment, such as at school and among friends. Around these general topics, each unit provides a variety of language items through a series of dialogues which serve as models of communicative language use and which in turn are supported by suggested activities, exercises, grammar explanations and cultural notes. Units are sub-divided into areas, each of which focuses on a specific aspect of the communicative activity. For example, where the general area of communicative activity of the unit is talking about clothing, the unit is divided into areas such as describing clothes, discussing how they look and what colour they are. Each unit also contains a Learn to Read section and is followed by a Learn to Write lesson.

A Chinese character gives little or no indication of its pronunciation. For this reason learning to read and write Chinese is one of the most challenging as well as one of the most fascinating aspects of learning the language. As an aid to students, *Hanyu pinyin* (the phonetic transcription of Chinese characters) is used throughout the course in the unit areas, where all new characters and all characters that have not appeared in any previous Learn to Read or Learn to Write sections of the course have the *pinyin* pronunciation written underneath them.

A key feature of the *Hànyǔ* materials is the integration of all aspects of the course and of the four macro skills of listening, speaking, reading and writing. The main texts in the units are the source from which come all the vocabulary items, characters, functions and notions, grammar and cultural infomation which together form the content of the course. All activities and exercises and the Learn to Read sections and Learn to Write lessons relate to these main texts so that the various elements of the course are fully integrated and serve to reinforce one another.

Hànyǔ for Intermediate Students Stage 1 Student's Book is accompanied by a *Practice Book* which contains both communicative activities and practice exercises in listening, speaking, reading and writing; cassette tapes which contain recordings of all texts, listening exercises (in both the *Student's Book* and the *Practice Book*) and texts from the Learn to Read sections and Learn to Write lessons; and a *Character Writing Book* for practising the characters from the Learn to Write lessons.

The *Teacher's Book* contains a comprehensive explanation of the methodology used in the *Hànyǔ for Intermediate Students Stage 1* course and sets out in detail the teaching sequence of all items occurring in the *Student's Book* and the *Practice Book*. It also provides more detailed notes on grammar and usage for teachers' reference, the texts of all listening exercises, suggested texts for writing tasks, and the solutions to all puzzles and word games.

When the revisions of the first two volumes of the *Hànyǔ* series are completed, the revised course will be as follows:

Hànyǔ for Beginning Students (based on *Hànyǔ 1*)
Hànyǔ for Intermediate Students Stage 1 (based on *Hànyǔ 1 & 2*)
Hànyǔ for Intermediate Students Stage 2 (based on *Hànyǔ 2*)
Hànyǔ for Intermediate Students Stage 3 (present *Hànyǔ 3*)
Hànyǔ for Senior Students (in planning stage)

Spacing of characters and use of *pinyin* in *Hànyǔ for Intermediate Students Stage 1*

Characters in Chinese script are normally written with even spacing. In *Hànyǔ for Intermediate Students Stage 1*, spaces have been inserted between words in the unit texts. For example:

我 喜欢 打 乒乓球。

Texts in the Learn to Read and Learn to Write sections are written conventionally, i.e. without spacing between words within a sentence. For example

我喜欢打乒乓球。

When *pinyin* is used to transcribe complete sentences, it is punctuated. For example:

Wǒ xǐhuan dǎ pīngpāngqiú.

When *pinyin* occurs as notation for pronunciation of individual characters, it is not punctuated. For example:

我 喜欢 听 古典 音乐。
wǒ xǐ   gǔdiǎn yuè

The use of *Hanyu pinyin* in *Hànyǔ for Intermediate Students Stage 1* conforms to the conventions set out in the document 汉语拼音正词法基本规则 (*Hànyǔ pīnyīn zhèngcífǎ jīběn guīzé*), dated 1 July 1988, issued by the State Education Committee and State Language Working Committee of the People's Republic of China and 现代汉语词典 (*Xiàndài Hànyǔ cídiǎn*) compiled by the Language Research Institute, Academia Sinica which lists the 'promotion of the standardisation of the Chinese language' as one of its aims and is widely regarded in the People's Republic of China as a standard reference on *pinyin*.

⊂⊃

This symbol denotes texts and listening exercises that are included on *Hànyǔ for Intermediate Students Stage 1 Cassettes*.

UNIT 1 What do you like doing?

第一单元
Dì-yī   dānyuán

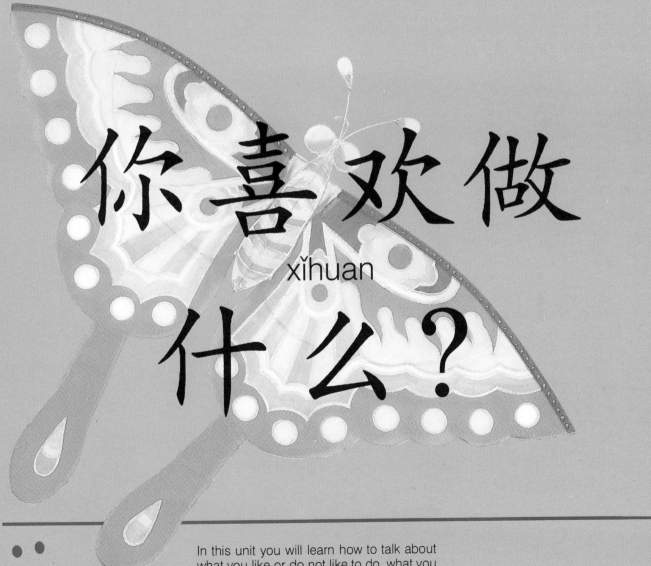

你喜欢做

xǐhuan

什么?

In this unit you will learn how to talk about what you like or do not like to do, what you can do, and how well or otherwise you do it. You will also learn how to telephone your friends!

1.1 Talking about your likes and dislikes

Chinese school children are usually involved in a lot of out-of-school activities. They like watching television and listening to radio programmes. Going to the movies is very popular (and very cheap). They read a lot and many are interested in dancing, painting or music.

Most schools have their own dance troupe, orchestra or choir and all students are encouraged to participate. Students may also go to the municipal Children's Palace and join one of many groups doing painting, singing, dancing, music or sports. There they can make use of the excellent facilities and receive expert instruction. It doesn't cost anything to join, but those who are accepted have to be good at their school work!

Much attention is given to physical fitness in Chinese schools and all students are encouraged to take part in sport activities. Many of these take place after school and at the end of the school day the schoolground will be filled with students and teachers jogging round the track, doing athletics or playing ball games.

To develop their skills further, students may join the local amateur sports school or a sports group at the Children's Palace.

● 你喜欢听音乐吗？
(Nǐ xǐhuan tīng yīnyuè ma?)

我 是 林 方。我 来 介绍 一下儿：
　　　　　　　　lái　jièshào

这 是 王 冰。
　　　　bīng

这 是 陈 华。
　　chén　huá

这 是 刘 新星。
　　liú　xīn

我 喜欢 唱 歌。
　xǐhuan　chàng gē

王 冰： 我 喜欢 听 音乐。
bīng　　　xǐhuan　tīng　yīnyuè

我 是 音乐迷。
yīnyuèmí

陈 华： 我 喜欢 画 画儿，
chén huá xǐhuan huà huàr

还 喜欢 养 动物。
xǐhuan dòngwù

我 养了 一 只 小 狗儿，
它 非常 可爱！
tā fēicháng ài

刘 新星： 我 呢，看 电视、看 电影、
liú xīn diànshì diànyǐng

跳舞，我 都 喜欢！
tiàowǔ dōu xǐhuan

王 冰，你 呢？
bīng

王 冰： 我 呀，也 喜欢 看 电视，
bīng ya xǐhuan diànshì

看 电影，听 音乐，跳舞。
diànyǐng tīng yīnyuè tiàowǔ

我 还 喜欢 出门 找 朋友。
xǐhuan chūmén zhǎo péngyou

刘 新星： 他 呀，最 爱 玩儿 了！
liú xīn ya zuì ài wánr

你喜欢吗？ 🔲

More activities — are they ones
you like doing?

买东西 mǎi dōngxi
玩儿电子游戏 wánr diànzǐ
yóuxì
吃东西 chī dōngxi
做饭 zuò fàn
上课 shàngkè
骑自行车 qí zìxíngchē
养猫 yǎng māo
打架 dǎjià

Find the Chinese

Let me introduce you, …
I also like keeping pets.
I like all of them.
He likes enjoying himself best!
I'm a music freak/music enthusi-
ast.
As for me …

Notes:

1. *Wǒ ne, kàn diànshì, kàn diànyǐng, tiàowǔ, wǒ dōu xǐhuan* — *Dōu* (都) is an adverb that has the meaning of 'all'. It 'sums up' the things that precede it — in this case, the activities of watching television, movies, dancing and visiting friends. Note that *dōu* never appears at the beginning of a sentence.

2. *Wǒ ya, yě xǐhuan kàn diànshì* — *Ā* (啊) when appearing after the syllables *a, e, i, o, ü* is influenced by these vowel sounds and becomes *ya* (呀) as a result. Used here in the middle of a sentence, it draws the listener's attention to the subject (As for me, I also like . . .)

Find the Chinese   →   page 3
怎么说？   →

Here's a summary of how you use the adverbs 都 (*dōu*), 也，不 and 很 in a sentence.

Tāmen	yě bú dōu yě bú dōu bú bù dōu	shì lǎoshī.

Tāmen	hěn yě hěn dōu hěn hěn bù	hǎo.

该你了！   →
你听懂了吗？   →   page 5

怎么说？

1. **他最爱玩儿了！**
   means 'His favourite activity is having a good time'. How would you say the following?
   a) I like dancing best.
   b) He likes watching television best.
   c) Her favourite activity is watching movies.
   d) She loves cycling best.
   e) They love keeping dogs.
   f) He enjoys getting into fights.

2. **我是音乐迷**
   means 'I'm mad about music' or 'I'm a music enthusiast'. How would you say you are mad about the following?
   a) novels
   b) movies
   c) rock music
   d) football

该你了！

How many sentences can you make up from the boxes on the left illustrating the use of 都，也，不 and 很? Write a list of sentences using all the combinations in the middle columns and substituting your own words in the first and third columns. Write the English meaning beside each of your sentences. Your sentences need not be true but they must make sense!

● 说汉语（一）

大卫：这是谁的 杂志？
　　　　　　　wèi　　zázhì

萨莉：是 我 的。
sàlì

大卫：你 也 喜欢 看 这个 杂志?!
　　　　　　　wèi　　xǐhuan　　　　zázhì

萨莉：是 啊，怎么 啦？
sàlì　　　a　　　la

大卫：我 最 喜欢 看 这个 杂志 了!
　　　　　zuì　xǐhuan　　　zázhì

　　　借 我 两 本 看看，可以 吗？
　　　　　　　　　　　　　　yǐ

萨莉：可以，你 要 哪 期 的？
　　　　yǐ

大卫：我 要 十二月 和 一月 的。
萨莉：好。
大卫：谢谢，我 下 星期 还(给) 你。
　　　　　　　　　　　huán gěi

Notes:

Zěnme la? — This is an often-heard phrase used when one is asking the reason for something. Hence, it means 'What's the matter?' or 'Why?' or 'What's up?' For example:

Tā zěnme la?　What's the matter with her?

Q:　*Nǐ xǐhuan tiàowǔ ma?*　Do you like to dance?
A:　*Xǐhuan, zěnme la?*　Yes, why do you ask?

Find the Chinese →

你听懂了吗？

(Nǐ tīngdǒng le ma?)

True or false?

1. a)　i)　Both girls like cats very much.
　　　ii)　Only one of the girls likes cats.
　　　iii)　They both dislike cats.
　b)　i)　The boy does not like animals.
　　　ii)　He does not like to keep pets.
　　　iii)　He does not mind keeping pets.

2. a)　i)　The group of people are all Japanese.
　　　ii)　Some of them are Japanese.
　　　iii)　Not all of them are Chinese.
　b)　i)　The girl said that the Japanese girl was not Hanako.
　　　ii)　She recognised Hanako when she saw her.

Find the Chinese

Yes, I do. Why?
December and January's.
Is it all right if I borrow two of them to read?
I'll return them next week.
Do you like this magazine too?
Which issues?

● 他们都喜欢运动！

(Tāmen dōu xǐhuan yùndòng!)

Jianhua's family are all sport enthusiasts. Here's what they like doing in their spare time.

姐姐：我 喜欢 打 篮球。
           xǐhuan   lán

妹妹：我 喜欢 打 乒乓球。
           xǐhuan   pīngpāng

弟弟：足球 最 有 意思 了！
       zú   zuì   yìsi

我 很 喜欢 踢 足球。
        xǐhuan tī zú

妈妈：我 不 太 喜欢 打 球。
            tài   xǐhuan

我 喜欢 跑步。
    xǐhuan   pǎobù

我 每 天 都 跑步。
          dōu   pǎobù

爸爸：我 喜欢 游泳，
       xǐhuan   yóuyǒng

我 常常 游泳。
  chángcháng   yóuyǒng

建华：我 也 喜欢 运动。
jiànhuá   xǐhuan   yùndòng

我 最 喜欢 打 排球。
    zuì   xǐhuan   pái

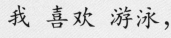

Find the Chinese

I go jogging every day.
Football is terrific!
We take exercise every day.
I don't like ball games much.
our whole family
I like playing football very much.
They all like sport.
I like playing volleyball best.

怎么说？

1. 我们一家人
   means 'our whole family'. How would you say the following?
   a) their whole family
   b) Mary's whole family
   c) Jianhua's whole family

2. How would you tell someone that your whole family likes the following?
   a) going out visiting friends
   b) watching movies
   c) swimming
   d) listening to music

3. 有意思
   is a way of describing an activity as 'interesting' or 'fun'. How would you say something is 'uninteresting' or 'boring'? How would you say the following?
   a) Football is boring.
   b) Tidying up the room is boring.

4. 最有意思了
   is an emphatic way of saying how interesting you think something is or what fun you think it is. How would you say the following?
   a) Swimming is the most fun!
   b) That magazine is the most interesting!

弟弟：我们 一 家 人 都 喜欢
　　　　　　　　　　dōu　xǐhuan

运动，我们 天天 锻炼 身体！
yùndòng　　　　　　duànliàn　shēntǐ

请问，你 喜欢 锻炼 身体 吗？
　　　　　　xǐhuan　duànliàn　shēntǐ

Notes:

1. *Wǒ xǐhuan dǎ lánqiú* — Dǎ (打) means 'to play' and refers to those ball games where one does not kick the ball — basketball, table tennis, volleyball and so on.
2. *Wǒ hěn xǐhuan tī zúqiú* — Tī (踢) means 'to kick', so *tī qiú* (踢球) is used when one is referring to games where the ball is kicked.
3. Note also that if you are using *yě* (也) and *hěn* (很) as Jianhua is doing when he says:

   Wǒ yě hěn xǐhuan yùndòng

   yě always comes before *hěn*.
4. *Wǒmen tiāntiān duànliàn shēntǐ* — Tiāntiān (天天) means 'every day', 'daily', or 'day in, day out' and is the same as 每天.

Find the Chinese → page 6
怎么说？ → page 6
Find your match →

你猜猜 →

没 意思！
　yìsi

Find your match!

你最喜欢做什么？
你最不喜欢做什么？

Find someone who thinks the same as you do. Go around the room asking people questions until you find someone who has the same tastes as you. When you find your partner, both sit down.

For example, you can ask:

Wǒ zuì xǐhuan/zuì ài tīng yīnyuè, nǐ ne?
Wǒ zuì bù xǐhuan zuò zuòyè, nǐ ne?

When someone asks you questions like this, you can reply:

Wǒ yě xǐhuan/yě zuì xǐhuan...
Wǒ bù xǐhuan/zuì bù xǐhuan...

When everyone who has found a partner is sitting down, one person from each pair should tell the class of their favourite likes and dislikes.

For example:

Wǒmen liǎng gè rén dōu xǐhuan/zuì bù xǐhuan...

你猜猜

Work with a partner. From the text and the list on page 8 choose the three sports you like to watch most and write them down in order of preference. Tell your partner your choices but not the order of preference. For example:

Wǒ xǐhuan kàn..., ... hé...

or

Wǒ xǐhuan kàn..., yě xǐhuan kàn...

Your partner must then guess which sport you like the most. For example:

Nǐ zuì xǐhuan kàn... ba?

or

Nǐ zuǐ xǐhuan kàn..., duì ma?

Qí zìxíngchē — The bicycle is one of the chief means of transport in China. A Chinese student would therefore not usually list bike riding as a leisure activity or hobby. Bicycles are considered rather as a practical means of getting from one place to another.

看书还是看电视？ 🔘

(Kàn shū háishi kàn diànshì?)

1. A: 你 喜欢 看 书 还是 看 电视？
       xǐhuan   diànshì

   B: 看书、看 电视，我 都 喜欢。
              diànshì   dōu xǐhuan

2. A: 你 喜欢 打 球 吗？
       xǐhuan

   B: 我 不 太 喜欢 打 球。
          tài xǐhuan

      我 喜欢 骑 自行车。
      xǐhuan qí

3. A: 安娜，你 呢？
       ānnà

   B: 我 不 喜欢 骑 自行车，
          xǐhuan qí

      骑 车 挺 累 的……。
      qí   lèi

你喜欢什么运动？ 🔘

Some more sporting activities:

打板球 dǎ bǎnqiú
 play cricket
打网球 dǎ wǎngqiú
 play tennis
打羽毛球 dǎ yǔmáoqiú
 play badminton
打壁球 dǎ bìqiú
 play squash
打棒球 dǎ bàngqiú
 play baseball
打曲棍球 dǎ qūgùnqiú
 play hockey
打保龄球 dǎ bǎolíngqiú
 play bowls
打太极拳 dǎ tàijíquán
 do taichi
踢橄榄球 tī gǎnlǎnqiú
 play rugby
做体操 zuò tǐcāo
 do gymnastics
做艺术体操 zuò yìshù tǐcāo
 do rhythmic gymnastics
做健身操 zuò jiànshēncāo
 do aerobics
跳水 tiàoshuǐ *dive, diving*
滑冰 huábīng *ice-skate, ice-skating*
滑雪 huáxuě *ski, skiing*
滑水 huáshuǐ *waterskiing*
溜滑板 liū huábǎn
 skateboarding
冲浪 chōnglàng *surf, surfing*
跳高 tiàogāo *(do) high jump*
跳远 tiàoyuǎn *(do) long jump*
跑步 pǎobù *jog, jogging*
骑自行车 qí zìxíngchē
 cycle, cycling
练武术 liàn wǔshù
 do martial arts
练瑜伽 liàn yúgā
 practise yoga
爬山 pá shān *mountain climbing*

我 最 喜欢 看 电视 了!
　　zuì　xǐhuan　　　diànshì

A: 我 知道，你

喜欢 看 电视，
xǐhuan　　　diànshì

还 喜欢 睡觉!
　　xǐhuan

Find the Chinese →
你听懂了吗? →

LEARN TO READ　page 28

LEARN TO WRITE　Lesson 1　page 38

Find the Chinese

Bike riding is quite/rather tiring.
I like both reading *and* watching
　television.
I like watching television best.

你听懂了吗?

(Nǐ tīngdǒng le ma?)

True or false?

1. a) The girl loves music, dance
　　　and sports.
　b) The girl loves music and
　　　dance but not sports.
　c) The girl loves sports but not
　　　music or dance.

2. a) She jogs every morning.
　b) She does a variety of exer-
　　　cises every morning.
　c) She does aerobics every
　　　morning.

3. a) The boy was quite eager to
　　　go jogging.
　b) The boy preferred not to go
　　　jogging.

1.2　Asking a '吗' question another way

● 你想不想去?
(Nǐ xiǎng bù xiǎng qù?)

A: 星期五 下午 你 有 没有 空儿?
B: 有 事儿 吗?
A: 你 想 不 想 去 看 电影?
　　xiǎng　　xiǎng　　　　　yǐng

B: 星期五 下午 我 有 事儿，
　　星期六 上午，行 吗?
A: 行。

B: 看 什么 电影?
　　　　yǐng

A: 这个 电影 好看 不 好看?
　　　　　　yǐng

B: 听说 不错。
　　tīng　　cuò

A: 那 咱们 就 看 这个 电影 吧!
　　　　　jiù　　　　　yǐng　ba

B: 好! 你 九 点 来 我 家,
　　　　　　　lái

咱们 坐 公共 汽车 去。
　　　gōnggòng　qì

A: 行。

Notes:

Nà zánmen jiù kàn zhèige diànyǐng ba! — 'In that case, let's watch this movie.' The adverb *jiù* (就) ushers in a result, in this case the result of the discussion.

Find the Chinese →

Here's another way you can form a general question:

Tā dà ma?	=	Tā	**dà bú dà?**
Tā lái ma?	=	Tā	**lái bù lái?**
Nà shì Bǐdé ma?	=	Nà	**shì bú shì** Bǐdé?
Tā yǒu qiúpāi ma?	=	Tā	**yǒu méiyǒu** qiúpāi?

When answering these questions, all you have to do is to answer in the affirmative or in the negative as the case may be. For example:

Tā qù bú qù?   *Tā qù.*
Nà shì bú shì Bǐdé?   *Shì, nà shì Bǐdé.*
Tā yǒu méiyǒu qiúpāi?   *Méiyǒu, tā méiyǒu qiúpāi.*

该你了! →

Find the Chinese

Is this film any good?
Is there something on?
Well, let's go and see this one then!
What film shall we go to?
How about Saturday morning?
All right.
Do you feel like going to see a movie?
Come to my place at 9 o'clock.
I've heard it's pretty good.
Okay, that's fine by me.

该你了!

1. Now see if you can rephrase these questions using the affirmative-negative form you have just learnt:
    a) *Tā shì Lǐ tàitai ma?*
    b) *Dīng xiǎojie de gǒu dà ma?*
    c) *Bǐdé de bàba xǐhuan yóuyǒng ma?*
    d) *Nǐmen jiā yǎng dòngwù ma?*
    e) *Nǐ hé nǐ dìdi dǎjià ma?*
    f) *Nǐ qù pǎobù ma?*
    g) *Nǐ yǒu zìxíngchē ma?*
    h) *Wáng lǎoshī tīng yīnyuè ma?*
    i) *Nèi běn xiǎoshuō hǎokàn ma?*
    Provide an answer to each question.

2. Role-play a scene where you and a friend have to decide on an activity — for example, going to see a movie. Some useful phrases you could use are:

    Asking if someone is free:
    XXX,你有空儿吗?

    Suggesting a time:
    ......, 行吗?

    Deciding:
    那咱们就......

那是不是丹尼？ 📼

调查一下儿！ **(Diàochá yíxiàr)**   →

LEARN TO READ   page 29

LEARN TO WRITE   Lesson 2   page 39

调查一下儿！

(Diàochá yíxiàr!)

Conduct a survey (调查 *diàochá*) of likes and dislikes in your class and report back. Different members of the class should survey different activities so that everyone is involved. One or two people could organise the results and write them up on the board.

Before beginning the survey, secretly note down your predictions of which activities will be most popular or least popular in your class. After the survey is completed, check how accurate your predictions were!

Tally the results by using the character 正.

1.3   Saying you've finished doing something

● 你带了几个球拍？ 📼

(Nǐ dàile jǐ gè qiúpāi?)

1. 李 明： 我 想 去 打 乒乓球。
   lǐ   pīngpāng

      你 去 不 去？

   张 云： 你 带 了 几 个 球拍？
   zhāng yún   dài   pāi

   李 明： 我 带 了 一 个。
   lǐ   dài

   张 云： 哦，我 没 有 带 球拍。
   zhāng yún   ò   dài   pāi

   李 明： 你 跟 小 华 借 吧。她 带 了。
            gēn   huá   dài

2. 张 云： 小华，借 我 球拍 用
　zhāng yún　　　　huá　　　　　　　pāi　yòng

一下儿 ，好 吗？

林 华： 你 想 借 我 的 球拍？
　lín huá　　　　　　　　　　　　pāi

我 的 杂志 你 还 没有
　　　　zázhì

还 呢！

张 云： 哦，对不起，
　　　ò

我 明天 还给 你，行 吗？

林 华： 好 吧。

张 云： 球拍 呢？
　　　pāi

林 华： 那，拿去 吧。
　　　　ná

Notes:

1. Wǒ de zázhì nǐ hái méiyǒu huán ne! — Note that wǒ de zázhì (我的杂志) is the object of the sentence. It is preposed, i.e. placed before the verb or, as in this case, before the subject, to emphasise it and make it conspicuous. This is done especially when the object is long and complicated. For example:

Nǐ gēge de qiúpāi jiè wǒ yòng yíxiàr, hǎo ma?

2. Qiúpāi ne? — You have previously learnt to use ne (呢) in sentences which contain an omission. For example: (Tā xǐhuan dǎ qiú.) Nǐ ne? Note that in this situation it is clear from the context what you are asking about. Ne can also be used when there is no context, in which case the speaker is asking where something or someone is. More examples:

Wǒ de zìxíngchē ne?　Where's my bike?
Nǐ mèimei ne?　Where's your sister?

Find the Chinese →
怎么说？ →
You are psychic! →

Find the Chinese

Will it be OK if I return it tomorrow?
Here, take it.
Borrow one from Xiao Hua.
How many bats did you bring?
Where's the bat?
I've brought one.
You still haven't returned my magazine!
Could I borrow your bat?

怎么说？

Note that Lin Hua says:

Wǒ de zázhì nǐ hái méiyǒu huán ne!

rather than

Nǐ hái méiyǒu huán wǒ de zázhì!

This is because she is feeling rather cross that Zhang Yun has not yet returned her magazine. By placing the object (i.e. the magazine) at the beginning of the sentence, it is stressed and the sentence sounds more forcible.

How would you complain to one of your classmates that he or she has not yet returned your:

- bicycle?
- brother's novel?
- Hanyu textbook?
- pingpong bat?
- Chinese magazine?

You are psychic!

Work in pairs. Together make a list of actions you may or may not have done the previous evening or that morning. You will each have a copy of the list. For example:

zuò zuòyè
chī zǎofàn
liù diǎn qǐchuáng
shōushi fángjiān
duànliàn shēntǐ

Both of you secretly tick or cross each item on your own list according to whether you did or did not do it. (This does not have to be true, but once you have put down a tick or a cross, you cannot change your mind later!) Now you take it in turn to test your psychic powers, by making statements about

Indicating an action is completed

1. When we want to indicate that an action is completed, we add *le* (了) immediately after the verb. For example:

   *Nǐ dài**le** shénme?*
   *Tāmen dōu lái**le**.* (They are all here.)
   *Shàng gè yuè wǒ kàn**le** sān běn shū.*
      (I read three books last month.)
   *Míngtiān wǎnshang wǒmen chī**le** fàn qù kàn diànyǐng.*
      (Tomorrow evening we'll go to the movies after dinner.)

   Notice that *le* (了) shows that the action is completed, but *not necessarily in the past*. The last example above refers to an action that is going to happen 'tomorrow evening'.
   When you are talking about *habitual* actions, you do not have to use *le*. For example:

   Qùnián wǒ měi tiān liù diǎn qǐchuáng. (Last year I got up at 6 every day.)
   Xiǎomíng chángcháng qù yóuyǒng.
      (Xiaoming often went swimming.)

   Also, when you are making a *simple statement of fact* (where the emphasis of the speaker is not on the completion or otherwise of the action), you do not have to use *le*.

   Tā zuótiān qù kàn diànyǐng. (She saw a movie yesterday.)
   Tā shàng (gè) xīngqī lái wǒ jiā.
      (He came to my home last week.)

   Note that if the verb takes an object after it (for example, to read novels — *kàn xiǎoshuō*), the object usually has before it a number and measure word, or something else to describe it. For example:

   *Wǒmen kàn**le** yì běn xiǎoshuō.*
   *Mǎlì jiè**le** nèi běn shū.*
   *Tā mǎi**le** Hànyǔ shū.*

   Otherwise, the statement is incomplete and would need some other element to complete its meaning. For example:

   *Wǒ kàn**le** diànshì jiù qù shuìjiào.*

2. Here is how you show that an action *has not* or *had not* been completed:

   *Wǒ **méi(yǒu)** qù.*

   or if you have not or had not done something *yet*:

   Wǒ hái méi(yǒu) chīfàn.

3. This is how you *ask* someone whether an action has been completed or not:

   *Nǐ qù**le méiyǒu?***
   *Nǐ chīfàn**le méiyǒu?***

what your partner did or did not do the previous evening or that morning. For example:

- *Nǐ zuótiān wǎnshang kànle diànyǐng.*
- *Nǐ zuótiān wǎnshang méiyǒu zuò zuòyè.*
- *Nǐ jīntiān zǎoshang chīle zǎofàn.*

If the 'psychic' is correct, the other person replies, for example:

   Duì, wǒ kànle diànyǐng.

If the 'psychic' is incorrect, the other person replies, for example:

   Bú duì, wo zuótiān wǎnshang méiyǒu kàn diànyǐng.

Now swap over! When you have finished, count up who was the best 'psychic'!

你听懂了吗？ 🔲

True or false?

1. a) i) The boy had not done his homework.
      ii) The boy had done his homework.
      iii) The boy was doing his homework.
   b) i) The word for XXX was . . .
      ii) The word for XXX was . . .
   c) i) The girl had not asked Teacher Zhang.
      ii) The girl was going to ask Teacher Zhang.
      iii) The girl had asked Teacher Zhang.

2. a) i) The boy was going to borrow a movie.
      ii) The boy had borrowed a movie.
      iii) The boy's brother had borrowed a movie.
   b) i) The girl had seen the movie.
      ii) The girl had heard about the movie.
   c) i) She will be going to the boy's home before lunch.
      ii) She will be going to the boy's home after lunch.

你听懂了吗？ →
借我，好吗？ → page 14

Who's here → page 14
LEARN TO READ page 30
LEARN TO WRITE Lesson 3 page 39

1.4   Saying what you can do

● 他 很 会 打 网球！ 📼

(Tā hěn huì dǎ wǎngqiú!)

王冰：　喂，你 现在 有 没有 空儿？
bīng　　wèi

陈华：　干 什么？
chén huá　　gàn

王冰：　咱们 去 打 网球 吧。
bīng　　　　　　　wǎng

陈华：　对不起，我 不 会 打
chén huá　　　　　　　　huì

网球。
wǎng

王冰：　没 关系，我 教 你。
　　　　　guānxi　　　jiāo

陈华：　我 现在 不 能 跟 你 去，
　　　　　　　　néng

我 得 去 找 李 老师。
děi　　zhǎo　lǐ

你 找 刘新 吧。
zhǎo　liú xīn

他 很 会 打 网球！
huì　　　wǎng

借我，好吗？

1. Make role-play exercises where:
   a) A asks B whether or not B has brought something to school. B has. A then asks to borrow the article and tells B when it will be returned.
   b) A asks B whether or not B has brought something to school. B has not. B then suggests someone else A could borrow the article from.
   c) A asks B to return something which was borrowed. B gives an excuse for not returning it. Here are some possible excuses:

我妈妈想看。
我还想看/用。
没有带。
我给了……了。

   A says when it must be returned!
2. Act out your role plays in front of the class or record your dialogues and listen to them.

Who's here?

Ask someone to check whether all members of your class are present today. They may:
- be present (来了)
- have not arrived yet (还没来)
- be not coming (不来了)

The person being asked may choose to do a roll-call. This is done by calling out each student's name to which he or she responds by calling out 'Dào (到)!' which literally means 'I've arrived'.

You can also respond by calling out 'Yǒu (有)!' (Here yǒu indicates existence.)

Find the Chinese →
怎么说？ →
你听懂了吗 →
Pass the parcel → page 16
What's your excuse? → page 16

● 说汉语（二）🔘

保罗： 你 能 帮 我 的 忙 吗?
bǎoluó　　　　néng　　　　　　máng

琳达： 什么 事儿?
líndá

保罗： 你 会 用 这个 程序 吗?
bǎoluó　　huì　　　　　　chéngxù

琳达： 会。怎么 啦?
líndá　　huì

保罗： 怎么 开始 啊?
　　　　　kāishǐ　　a

琳达： 老师 今天 上午 讲 了。
　　　　　　　　　　　jiǎng

保罗： 我 知道 他 讲 了。
　　　　　　　　jiǎng

可是，我 还
不 会!
　　huì

你 能 教教 我 吗?
néng　jiāojiāo

Find the Chinese

That doesn't matter, I'll teach you.
Why don't you go and ask Liu Xin?
Are you free just now?
I can't go with you just now.
I have to go and see Mr Li.
He's very good at tennis.
I don't know how to play tennis.
What do you want?

duō

怎么说？

1.　会 is how you say you can do something because you *know how* to do it. How would you say that you can do the following?
　　a)　swim
　　b)　speak Chinese
　　c)　play football

2.　能 is how you say you can or cannot do something for some reason (often physical). For example, if you had a bad cold, you might tell your friends.

　　　我今天不能游泳。

How would you tell a friend that you cannot do the following?
　　a)　play tennis this afternoon (You have to see Mr Smith)
　　b)　go to the movies this evening (You have to catch up on your homework)
　　c)　play pingpong just now (You have to tidy up the room)

你听懂了吗? 🔘

True or false?

1.　a)　The woman wanted to help the boy and girl.
　　b)　She needed help.
　　c)　She wanted to practise her English.

2.　a)　The woman spoke no English at all.
　　b)　She could speak some English.
　　c)　She could speak English fluently.

琳达： 好。你 先 打 "w" 和 "p"
líndá   xiān

两 个 字母，然后 按 这个
     mǔ   ránhoù   àn

键。
jiàn

保罗： 哦，挺 容易 的！
bǎoluó   ò   róngyì

琳达： 是 啊。你 试 一 试。
           a   shì   shì

保罗： 先 打 "w" 和 "p" 两 个 字母，
      xiān   mǔ

然后 按 这个 键。
ránhoù   àn   jiàn

琳达： 对了！

Notes:

Nǐ shì yí shì — This is the same as *shìshì* (试试). When a single syllable verb is reduplicated, *yī* （一） may be inserted between the two syllables.

Find the Chinese →

LEARN TO READ   page 32

LEARN TO WRITE   Lesson 4   page 40

Pass the parcel

A mystery parcel is made up containing descriptions of someone who is good at something. The descriptions could be contributed by members of the class. For example:

Hěn huì chàng gē.
Hěn huì tī zúqiú.
Hěn huì tiàowǔ.

The parcel is passed around in a circle while music plays. When the music stops, the person who receives the parcel unwraps the top layer and reads out the label, then gives it to the person he or she considers most appropriate. The parcel cannot be given to the same person more than once.

What's your excuse?

Act out a role play where you suggest doing something with friends and they refuse because they have to do something else. Some phrases you can use are:

Zánmen qù..., hǎo ma?
Duìbuqǐ, wǒ xiànzài bù néng gēn nǐ qù. Wǒ děi (qù)...

Find the Chinese

How do you begin?
What do you want (me to help you with)?
But I still can't do it!
Yes, I can. Why (do you ask)?
Then you press this key.
Could you help me, please?
That's right!
I know he told us about it.
First you type the two letters...
Do you know how to use this program?

1.5 Describing actions

● 她画得非常好！

(Tā huà de fēicháng hǎo!)

1. 兰兰： 你们 自己 介绍 一下儿 吧。
   lánlán   jǐ   jièshào

   丁 力： 我 叫 丁 力。
   dīng lì   dīng lì

   马 小青： 我 叫 马 小青。
   mǎ   qīng   mǎ   qīng

   白 云： 我 叫 白 云。
   bái yún   bái yún

2. 兰兰： 丁 力 喜欢 游泳。
        dīng lì   yóuyǒng

   他 游 得 很 快！
       yóu de

3. 马 小青： 我 喜欢 画 画儿。
   mǎ   qīng   huà huàr

   兰兰： 她 很 会 画 画儿。
   lánlán   huà huàr

   她 画 得 非常 好。
      huà de

   你 说，她 画 得 怎么样？
          huà de

她 的 字 写 得 怎么样?

她 的 字
写 得 太 乱 了!
xiě de   luàn

Notes:

1. In Chinese, some words that denote actions are actually verb-object constructions, i.e. they are made up of a verb and an object. For example:

> *yóuyǒng* (to swim) = *yóu* (to swim) + *yǒng* (a swim)
> *huà huà(r)* (to draw, paint) = *huà* (to draw, paint) + *huà(r)*
>   (drawing, painting)
> *kàn shū* (to read) = *kàn* (to look) + *shū* (a book)
> *zǒulù* (to walk) = *zǒu* (to walk) + *lù* (road)
> *tiàowǔ* (to dance) = *tiào* (to dance) + *wǔ* (a dance)
> *chàng gē* (to sing) = *chàng* (to sing) + *gē* (song)

When such verbs are followed by an object, the 'object' part of the verb-object construction is omitted. For example:

> *Tā kàn xiǎoshuō.*

This is also the case if the verb is followed by a complement (a word used to explain or complete the meaning of the verb. See note 2 below.)

2. *Tā yóu de zhēn kuài* — When you wish to describe the extent to which someone does something, the description is placed immediately *after* the verb, and is linked to the verb with *de* (得). *De* and the description is called a complement of degree.

Subject	verb	complement of degree	
Tā	yóu	得	hěn kuài.

Here's how you can ask how well someone swims and some possible answers:

Tā	**yóu**	**de**	**zěnmeyàng*?**
Tā	**yóu**	**de**	hěn kuài.
		de	bú tài hǎo.
		de	fēicháng màn.

* You have met *zěnmeyàng* before in sentences such as:

  Nǐ zěnmeyàng? Hǎo ma? and *Jīntiān tiānqì zěnmeyàng?*

Zěnmeyàng means 'how' and may be used when asking for information regarding the quality of something, the situation, or the way in which something is done. For example:

  Nǐmen de Hànyǔ lǎoshī zěnmeyàng? How's your Chinese language teacher?
  Nèi běn shū zěnmeyàng? How was the book?
  Nǐmen shàngkè shàng de zěnmeyàng? How was the lesson?

你说中国话说得怎么样？
(Nǐ shuō Zhōngguóhuà shuō de zěnmeyàng?)

1.

他 打 字
打 得 很 慢。
  de   màn

2.

她 唱 歌
chàng gē

唱 得 真 好听。
chàng de

3.

他 吃 饭
吃 得 很 高兴。
  de   gāoxìng

4.

王 先生 跳舞
   xiān   tiàowǔ

跳 得 不 太 好。
tiào de

5.

你 觉得 她 说 中国话
　　jué

说 得 怎么样?
　　de

她 说 得 非常 流利!
　　de　　　　liúlì

6.

他 游泳
　　yóuyǒng

游 得 非常 快!
yóu de

他 游 得 更 快。
yóu de gèng

他 游 得 最 快 了!
yóu de

Notes:

When you are describing how someone is doing something and the verb in the sentence takes an object (e.g. *dǎ páiqiú*), the verb must be repeated after the object. For example:

| Tā | **dǎ** | páiqiú | **dǎ** | de | hěn hǎo. |
| Tā | **qí** | zìxíngchē | **qí** | de | hěn kuài. |

Note that this also applies to those verbs that are actually verb-object constructions, such as

tiàowǔ (to dance) = *tiào* (to dance) + *wǔ* (a dance)
yóuyǒng (to swim) = *yóu* (to swim) + *yǒng* (a swim)

If you want to use these verbs in full, you must repeat the verb after the object:

Ta **tiào**wǔ **tiào** de hěn hǎo.
Tā **yóu**yǒng **yóu** de hěn kuài.

Here's how you ask how someone is doing something:

| Tā tiàowǔ | **tiào de zěnmeyàng?** |

Here's how you can vary your descriptions of what someone is doing:

Tā huà de	fēicháng	hǎo.
	zhēn	hǎo.
	hěn	hǎo.
	tǐng	hǎo (de).
	bú tài	hǎo.
	bù	hǎo.
	hěn bù	hǎo.

You can also make comparisons in your descriptions:

Wǒ juéde tā huà de	hěn	hǎo.
	gèng	
	zuì	

你听懂了吗？ →
Calligraphy contest →

● 我明白了！ 🔲
(Wǒ míngbai le!)

1. 小明： (to Mary) 你 打 得 真 好！
de

约汉： 是，她 很 会 打 球。
yuēhàn

玛丽： 哪里，哪里。
mǎlì   li   li

小明： (to Mary) 你 喜欢 打 篮球 吗？
lán

玛丽： 喜欢。网球、篮球、
mǎlì   wǎng   lán

排球、我 都 喜欢。
pái

你听懂了吗？ 🔲

True or false?

1. a) Xiaoming and Mark were there because they wanted to dance.
   b) They were there because they had little else to do.

2. a) Mark had learnt to dance before.
   b) Mark has never learnt to dance.
   c) Mark is extremely good at dancing.

3. a) Linda is a beginner at dancing.
   b) Linda is probably quite a good dancer.

Calligraphy contest
书法比赛

Organise a calligraphy (书法 shūfǎ) contest (比赛 bǐsài) in the class. Each student prepares a specimen of writing, and all entries are placed on display. Members of the class form small groups in which they discuss the entries (see the boxes on this page for possible comments) and decide which one they think is best. For example:

我觉得XX写得真好看。
我觉得XX写得更好。

When the discussions are completed, the votes are taken and the entry that is voted the best is declared the winner.

XX同学说XX写得最好。

小明：　哦，看来，你 是 球迷！
　　　　ò　　　　　　　　　 mí

　　　　(to John) 你 呢？

　　　　你 也 喜欢 体育 运动 吗？
　　　　　　　　tǐyù　　yùndòng

约汉：　我？ 我 不 喜欢 体育 运动。
yuēhàn　　　　　　　　 tǐyù　 yùndòng

　　　　我 喜欢 跳舞。
　　　　　　　 tiàowǔ

玛丽：　他 很 会 跳舞！
mǎlì　　　　　　 tiàowǔ

约汉：　我 也 喜欢 听 音乐。
yuēhàn　　　　　　　　 yīnyuè

小明：　你 喜欢 听 什么 音乐？
　　　　　　　　　　　 yīnyuè

约汉：　古典·音乐。
　　　　gǔdiǎn　yīnyuè

玛丽：　我 最 不 喜欢 古典 音乐 了！
mǎlì　　　　　　　　 gǔdiǎn　yīnyuè

　　　　我 喜欢 摇滚乐。
　　　　　　　 yáogǔnyuè

小明：　你们 俩 是 好 朋友……
　　　　　　 liǎ　　　 péngyou

　　　　可是 一 个 喜欢 运动，
　　　　　　　　　　　　 yùndòng

一 个 不 喜欢 ; 一 个 喜欢

古典 音乐 , 一 个 喜欢
gǔdiǎn yīnyuè

摇滚乐 。
yáogǔnyuè

玛丽 ： 哦 ， 那 没 什么 ，
mǎlì ò

我 最 喜欢 看 约汉 跳舞 了 。
yuēhàn tiàowǔ

他 跳 得 真 好 ！
tiào de

约汉 ： 我 呢 ， 我 有 空儿 就 来 看
yuēhàn jiù

她 打 球 ！ 她 打 球 打 得 可
de

好 了 ！

小明 ： 哦 ， 原来 如此 ！ 我 明白 了 ！
ò yuánlái rúcǐ bai

Find the Chinese

Do you like sport too?
So that's how it is !
I get it!
He's very good at dancing.
What kind of music do you like?
I hate classical music!
One of you likes sport and the other one doesn't.
It looks like you're mad about ball games.
Oh, that's nothing.
Whenever I'm free I come and watch her play.
You two are good friends.
She plays wonderfully!

哪里 , 哪里 。

Work with a partner. You and your partner take it in turns to pay each other a compliment.
For example:

Nǐ chàng gē chàng de hěn hǎotīng!

See who can think up the most compliments and so keep going the longest.
Note that:
- The person receiving a compliment must respond:

  Nǎli, nǎli.

- The compliment need not be true!

Notes:
Nǐmen liǎ — Liǎ （俩） is a colloquial way of saying *liǎng gè* (two of …).
Nǐmen liǎ means 'the two of you'. Also: *zánmen liǎ, tāmen liǎ.*

Find the Chinese →
哪里 , 哪里 →

LEARN TO READ page 33
LEARN TO WRITE Lesson 5 page 41

1.6   Telephoning your friends

● 我 最 喜 欢 给 朋 友 打 电 话 了！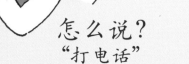

(Wǒ zuì xǐhuan gěi péngyou dǎ diànhuà le!)

这 是 我 的 电 话 簿。
                   huà bù

这些 是 我 朋友 的 电话 号码。
xiē   péngyou   huà   mǎ

琳达 的 电话 号码 是 870 6592。
líndá   huà   mǎ

我 最 喜欢 给 朋友 打 电话 了！
             péngyou   huà

我 的 电话 号码 是 302 1147。
     huà   mǎ

请问，你 的 电话 号码 是 多少？
              huà   mǎ

怎么说?
"打电话" means 'to telephone' and

"给……打(个)电话" means 'to telephone (someone)'. How would you say that you are going to telephone the following people?
- your sister
- your brother
- Mary
- Martin
- Liu Fang
- your teacher

For example, you could say:

我要给我哥哥打(个)电话。

我的电话簿

Make a 'telephone book' (diànhuà-bù). Write down the names of any ten students whose telephone numbers you do *not* know already, then go and ask these students (in Chinese) what their telephone numbers are. List the numbers in your book. You will also be replying to enquiries about what *your* telephone number is.

Remember that when you are expressing telephone numbers, you say them in 'telephone style', i.e. each number is said individually. Remember, also, to express 'one' as 幺 yāo.

Notes:

1. 8706592 — When expressing a telephone number, each digit is read out individually (bā-qī-líng-liù-wǔ-jiǔ-èr).

2. Sān-líng-èr-yāo-yāo-sì-qī—Yī (一) is often read out as yāo (幺) for the sake of clarity.

怎么说? →
我的电话簿 →

● 你的电话号码是多少？

(Nǐ de diànhuà hàomǎ shì duōshao?)

1. 安娜： 明天 我 和 阿伦，劳拉
   ānnà
   ālún   láolā

   想 去 游泳，你 也 去 吧！

   马丁： 游泳？我 不 去。
   mǎdīng

   安娜：怎么 啦？

   马丁： 我 游 得 不 好。

   安娜： 没 关系。我 也 不 太 会 游泳。
   guānxi

   马丁： 明天 什么 时候？
   shíhou

   安娜：下午 一 点 半。

   马丁： 一 点 半？我 不 知道 明天 下午
   家里 有 没有 事儿。⋯⋯ 这样
   吧，我 明天 早上 给 你 打 一 个
   电话，好 吗？

   安娜： 好。几 点？

   马丁： 上午 九 点。

   安娜： 好。

马丁：　你　的　电话　号码　是　多少？
mǎdīng　　　　　　　　　　　mǎ

安娜：　275 3104。
ānnà

马丁：　275 3…。请　你　再　说　一　遍。
　　　　　　　　　　　　　　　　　biàn

安娜：　275 3104。

马丁：　275 3-1-0-4。

安娜：　对。

2. 妈妈：　喂？
　　　　　wèi

马丁：　哦，伯母，您　好！我　是　马丁。
　　　　ò　bómǔ　nín　　　　　　mǎdīng

妈妈：　你　好，马丁！

马丁：　请　安娜　接　电话，好　吗？
　　　　　　ānnà　jiē

妈妈：　她　不　在　家。她　去　找　玛丽
　　　　　　　　　　　　　　　　mǎlì

了，一会儿　回来。

马丁：　请　您　让　她　给　我　回　电话，
　　　　　nín　ràng　　　　　　　　huà

好　吗？

妈妈：　好。

马丁：　谢谢！

Find the Chinese

Martin just telephoned you.
Why not?
How about if I give you a ring tomorrow morning?
Could you get her to ring me back, please?
I'm not sure whether or not we're doing anything at home tomorrow afternoon.
Could I speak to Anna, please?
She'll be back soon.
Why don't you come too?
What's your telephone number?
It's 275-3104.
Could you say that again, please.
She's gone to Mary's.
When tomorow?
I can't swim very well either.
He wants you to ring back.
I'll ring him back now.

3. 妈妈： 安娜，马丁 刚才
   　　　　ānnà　　mǎdīng　gāngcái

   给 你 打 了 一 个 电话。
   　　　　　　　　　　　huà

   安娜： 什么 时候？
   　ānnà　　shíhou

   妈妈： 九 点 一 刻。他 让 你
   　　　　　　　　kè　　　ràng

   回 电话。
   　　huà

   安娜： 好。我 现在 就 给 他 回
   　　　　　　　　　jiù

   电话。
   huà

Notes:

1. *Tā ràng nǐ huí diànhuà* — *Ràng* (让) means 'to ask (somebody to do something)'. More examples:

   Nǐ ràng tā zhǎo wǒ.
   Nǐ ràng tā lái ba!

2. *Wǒ xiànzài jiù gěi tā huí diànhuà* — The adverb *jiù* (就) can be used to indicate that the action happens soon, or quickly, as in this case.

Find the Chinese → page 26
打电话 →
你听懂了吗？ →

● 说汉语（三）

Suppose you are Martin. Together with a classmate, make up a telephone conversation informing Anna of your decision. Role-play your telephone conversation. You have the following options:

1. *Wǒ néng qù.*　　But you have to arrange a different time to meet Anna.

2. *Wǒ bù néng qù.*　a) You have to help someone do something, or
   　　　　　　　　b) You have to finish a long overdue homework assignment.

LEARN TO READ page 34
LEARN TO WRITE Lesson 6 page 42

打电话

Work in pairs.

1. Role-play telephoning a friend and leaving a message for him or her. when you find your friend is not home.

2. Role-play a telephone conversation between Mary and John in which they decide how to spend the coming Saturday afternoon.

你听懂了吗？

True or false?

1. a) David was speaking to Linda on the phone.
   b) Mary was speaking to David.
   c) Linda was speaking to Peter.

2. a) The phone number David found was the right number.
   b) It was the wrong number.

3. a) Jenny would probably have the number Linda wanted.
   b) It's not at all clear whether Jenny has the number.

你 是 玛丽 吗？

你 打错 电话 了
　　cuò　　huà

学会认字 (Xuéhuì rèn zì)

1.1

Before reading the text, listen to the recording and answer the questions.

Text 1
True or false?
1. The speaker is having a chat with his friends.
2. He is giving a talk about his family.
3. His parents are both teachers.
4. His parents are keen on sports.

Text 2
True or false?
1. The girl and boy are discussing the merits of a novel.
2. The girl wants to borrow the novel.
3. The girl has about a week to read the novel.

● 汉字表

都
喜
欢
常
电
视
最
非
以
还

		As in
dōu	all	他们都喜欢
xǐ	to like; be fond of	喜欢
huān	joyous; merry	
cháng	often	常常；非常
diàn	electricity; electric	电视
shì	to look at	
zuì	most	最大；最好
fēi	not; no	非常
yǐ	according to	可以
huán	to return	还书

Text 🔊

1.　　老师好,同学们好！我叫王亚文,
今年十三岁,是中学生。

我家有四个人，爸爸、妈妈、弟弟和我。

我爸爸是老师，妈妈也是老师。他们都喜欢看书和打球。星期六下午他们常常去打球。

我和弟弟都喜欢看书，看电视，也喜欢打球。我还喜欢养狗。我弟弟最喜欢看电视。

对了，他还喜欢睡觉！

2. G: 这是谁的小说？

　　B: 是我的。

　　G: 这本小说好看吗？

　　B: 很好看。我非常喜欢看这本小说。

　　G: 借我看看，可以吗？

　　B: 可以。

　　G: 谢谢，下星期还你。

　　B: 好。

动动脑筋

(Dòngdong nǎojīn)

What do you think these are?

1. 电车
2. 电笔

1.2

Before reading the text, listen to the recording and answer the questions.

True or false?
1. The girl came to see the boy about going to see a movie.
2. The boy has seen the movie before.
3. The boy was busy on Saturday but said he would go.
4. They decided to meet at the cinema.

● 汉字表

			As in
影	yǐng	shadow	电影
想	xiǎng	to think; want	想看电影
听	tīng	to listen	听说

太	tài	extremely, too	太好了!
公	gōng	public	公共汽车
共	gòng	common; altogether	
汽	qì	steam; vapour	汽车
样	yàng	appearance; shape	怎么样?
来	lái	to come	来我家
吧	ba	(modal particle)	你来我家吧

Text 📻

G: 星期六早上你有没有事儿?

B: 没事儿。

G: 咱们去看电影,好吗?

B: 好,看什么电影?

G: (points to ad in newspaper)

我想看这个电影。
听说这个电影非常好看。

B: 太好了,我也想看这个电影。
咱们怎么去?

G: 坐公共汽车去,怎么样?

B: 好。星期六你来我家还是我去你
家?

G: 星期六早上九点,你来我家吧。

B: 好,星期六见!

动动脑筋

(Dòngdong nǎojīn)

Give an example of each of the
following.

1. 公路
2. 公事

1.3

Before reading the text, listen to the recording and answer the questions.

True or false?
1. The girl was studying Chinese.
2. The boy didn't have a textbook.
3. The boy borrowed the girl's Chinese textbook.
4. Xiao Ming had done his Chinese homework.

● 汉字表

As in

用	yòng	*to use*	借我用
带	dài	*to bring*	带汉语课本
跟	gēn	*(preposition) with; and*	跟他借
啦	la	*(fusion of 了 and 啊)*	怎么啦？
行	xíng	*OK; be all right*	行吗？
拿	ná	*to take*	拿去吧。

Text

大同： 你的汉语课本借我用一下
儿,好吗？

林方： 对不起,我正在用呢。
你的汉语课本呢？

大同： 我没有带。

林方： 你跟小明借吧。
我去问问他。
小明,汉语作业你做了吗？

小明： 做了,怎么啦？

林方： 大同没带他的汉语课本。
你的汉语课本可以借给他
用一下儿吗？

小明： 行。拿去吧。

动动脑筋

(Dòngdong nǎojīn)

1. Give three examples of this.

常用字

2. What would you think of some-one who is good at doing this?

用人

1.4

Before reading the text, listen to the recording and answer the questions.

True or false?
1. The boy and the girl are in the same grade.
2. The boy was going to Teacher Wang for help with his schoolwork.
3. The girl offered to help him with his homework.
4. She is a good tutor.

● 汉字表

空干啊得找会容易能			As in
	kòng	empty; spare time	有空儿
	gàn	to do	干什么?
	a	(indicating questioning tone)	咱们去啊?
	děi	must; have to	我得去
	zhǎo	to look for	找老师
	huì	to know how to; can	会做作业
	róng	to permit; allow	容易
	yì	easy	
	néng	can; be able to	能跟我打球

Text ⊙⊙

1. a) G: 下午你有空儿吗?

   B: 干什么?

   G: 咱们去打球吧?

   B: 不行,下午我得去找王老师。

   b) G: 你找王老师干什么?

   B: 今天的课,我还不会呢!

   G: 我会,我可以帮你。

   B: 你现在有空儿吗?

   G: 有,现在我可以帮你。

   B: 太好了!

动动脑筋

(Dòngdong nǎojīn)

1. If you had thought up plans that were described as

   空想,

   would you be happy?

2. Somebody is said to be a

   能人。

   What do you think he or she is?

2. G: 你现在懂了吗？

   B: 懂了。挺容易的。谢谢你。

   G: 不谢。怎么样，你现在能跟我打球吗？

   B: 可以。走啊！

1.5

Before reading the text, listen to the recording and answer the questions.

True or false?
1. Both Xiao Ming and his brother are excellent swimmers.
2. Xiao Ming's brother is a better swimmer.
3. Xiao Ming's family are well known as a family of sports enthusiasts.
4. Judging from what was said, there are five persons in Xiao Ming's family.

● 汉字表

			As in
游	yóu	to swim	游泳
更	gèng	more; even more	更快；更好
泳	yǒng	to swim	游泳
体	tǐ	body	体育
育	yù	to educate; bring up	
运	yùn	motion; movement	运动
动	dòng	to move	
跑	pǎo	to run	跑步
步	bù	step	
得	de	(structural particle)	跑得很快
之	zhī	(auxiliary word)	体育之家

Text 📼

1. B: 那是谁啊？

   G1: 小明的弟弟。

B: 他游得真快！

小明和他的弟弟，谁游得快？

G1: 小明游得更快。

G2: 他们两个兄弟游泳都游得非常好。

2. B: 听说，他们一家人都喜欢体育运动。

G1: 是的，他们一家人都喜欢体育运动。小明的爸爸、妈妈打球打得非常好。他哥哥跑步，也跑得挺快的。

G2: 他们家的狗也跑得很快！

B: 是吗？他们真是个"体育之家"！

动动脑筋

(Dòngdong nǎojīn)

People driving vehicles called

跑车

attract a great deal of attention. What do you think these vehicles are?

1.6

Before reading the text, listen to the recording and answer the questions.

True or false?
1. Lin Fang was not at home.
2. Wang Xiaoming phoned to ask when Lin Fang was returning home.
3. Wang's phone number is 275 3864.
4. Lin Fang decided to return the call at once.

● 汉字表

			As in
时	shí	*time*	时候
候	hòu	*time; season*	
朋	péng	*friend*	朋友
友	yǒu	*friend*	
话	huà	*words; remark*	电话
让	ràng	*to let; allow*	让他给我打电话
刚	gāng	*just; only a short while ago*	刚才
才	cái	*then (and only then)*	
就	jiù	*at once; right away*	现在就打电话

Text

1. B1: 林方在家吗？

   G: 不在，他去学校了。

   B1: 你知道他什么时候回来吗？

   G: 不知道。

   B1: 我是他的朋友王小明。
   请你让他给我回电话，
   好吗？

   G: 好，你的电话是多少号？

   B1: 二五七 - 三九六四。

   G: 二五七 - 三九六四。

   B1: 对了，谢谢你！

   G: 不谢。

2. G: 林方，王小明刚才给你打电话了。
   他让你回电话。

   B2: 好，谢谢。
   我现在就给他回电话。

动动脑筋

(Dòngdong nǎojīn)

1. Where would you find this?

   公用电话

2. What is this?

   电动车

SUMMARY

(LTR stands for Learn to Read; LTW stands for Learn to Write)

1.1 Talking about your likes and dislikes

Now you can:

talk about likes and dislikes:
Wǒ xǐhuan chàng gē. 我喜欢唱歌。
Tā zuì ài wánr le! 他最爱玩了!
Wǒ hěn xǐhuan tīng yīnyuè. 我很喜欢听音乐。
Wǒ bú tài xǐhuan dǎ qiú. 我不太喜欢打球。

express your enthusiasm:
Zúqiú zuì yǒu yìsi le! 足球最有意思了!
Wǒ zuì xǐhuan kàn zhèige zázhì le! 我最喜欢看这个杂志了!

ask if you can borrow or return some magazines and say when you will return them:
Jiè wǒ liǎng běn (zázhì) kànkan, kěyǐ ma? 借我两本(杂志)看看,可以吗?
Wǒ xià gè xīngqī huán(gěi) nǐ. 我下个星期还(给)你。

ask which issue of a magazine someone wants:
Nǐ yào něi qī de? 你要哪期的?

possible reply:
Wǒ yào shí'èryuè hé yīyuè de. 我要十二月和一月的。

say how often you do something:
Wǒ měi tiān dōu pǎobù. 我每天都跑步。
Wǒ chángcháng yóuyǒng. 我常常游泳。

say which is your favourite sport:
Wǒ zuì xǐhuan dǎ páiqiú. 我最喜欢打排球。

ask someone their preferences:
Nǐ xǐhuan kàn shū háishi kàn diànshì? 你喜欢看书还是看电视?

Useful phrases
Zěnme la? 怎么啦? *Why do you ask?*
Méi yìsi. 没意思。 *It's boring.*
Kěyǐ. 可以。 *Yes (you may; you can).*
(LTW) tóng yí gè xuéxiào 同一个学校 *the same school*

Extra vocabulary
More activities   page 3
More sporting activities   page 8

1.2 Asking a '吗' question another way

Now you can:

ask a '吗' question another way:
Nǐ xiǎng bù xiǎng qù kàn diànyǐng? 你想不想去看电影?
Nǐ yǒu méiyǒu kòngr? 你有没有空儿?
Zhèige diànyǐng hǎokàn bù hǎokàn? 这个电影好看不好看?

make a decision:
Nà wǒmen jiù kàn zhèige diànyǐng ba! 那我们就看这个电影吧!

Useful phrases
Xíng. 行。 *OK. All right.*
..., xíng ma? ......行吗? *Is...all right? Will...be all right?*
Búcuò. 不错。 *Pretty good. Not bad.*

1.3 Saying you've finished doing something

Now you can:

ask someone about an action that's been completed:
Nǐ dàile jǐ gè qiúpāi? 你带了几个球拍?

possible replies:
Wǒ dàile yí gè. 我带了一个。
Wǒ méiyǒu dài qiúpāi. 我没有带球拍。

suggest who to borrow something from:
Nǐ gēn Xiǎo Huá jiè ba. 你跟小华借吧。

complain to someone about not returning something:
Wǒ de zázhì nǐ hái méiyǒu huán ne! 我的杂志你还没有还呢!

Useful phrases
Hái méiyǒu. 还没有。 *Not yet.*
Hǎo ba. 好吧。 *All right. (agreeing to something)*
Nà, náqu ba. 那,拿去吧。 *Here, take it.*

1.4 Saying what you can do

Now you can:

ask someone if they know how to do something:
Nǐ huì yòng zhèige chéngxù ma? 你会用这个程序吗?

say you are unable or it is not possible for you to do something:
Wǒ xiànzài bù néng gēn nǐ qù. 我现在不能跟你去。

and give the reason why:
Wǒ děi qù zhǎo lǎoshī 我得去找老师。

say someone is good at something:
Tā hěn huì dǎ wǎngqiú! 他很会打网球!

ask someone if they can help you with something:
Nǐ néng bāng wǒ de máng ma? 他能帮我的忙吗?

explain how to work something on a computer program:
Nǐ xiān dǎ "W" hé "P" liǎng gè zìmǔ. Ránhòu àn zhèige jiàn. 你先打 "W" 和 "P" 两个字母，然后按这个键。

Useful phrases
Gàn shénme? 干什么? *Why? What for?*
Shì yí shì. 试一试。 *Try. Have a go.*
Shénme shìr? 什么事儿? *What's happening?*
Duì le! 对了! *That's right!*
(LTW) zhème wǎn 这么晚 *so late*

1.5 Describing actions

Now you can:

describe actions:
Tā hěn huì huà huàr. 她很会画画儿。
Tā chàng de hěn hǎotīng. 她唱得很好听。
Tā tiàowǔ tiào de bú tài hǎo. 他跳舞跳得不太好。
Tā dǎzì dǎ de hěn màn. 他打字打得很慢。
Tā shuō de fēicháng liúlì. 他说得非常流利。
Tā de zì xiě de tài luàn le! 他的字写得太乱了!

compare actions:
Tā yóu de gèng kuài. 他游得更快。
Tā yóu de zuì kuài. 他游得最快。

ask someone's opinion about someone's actions:
Nǐ juéde tā shuō Zhōngguóhuà shuō de zěnmeyàng? 你觉得他说中国话说得怎么样?
Nǐ shuō, tā huà de zěnmeyàng? 你说,他画得怎么样?

Useful phrases
Nǎli, nǎli. 哪里，哪里。 *(polite response to praise)*
Nà méi shénme. 那没什么。 *No problem. That's nothing.*
Yuánlái rúcǐ. 原来如此。 *So that's how it is. Oh, I see.*

1.6 Telephoning your friends

Now you can:

ask for someone's telephone number:
Nǐ de diànhuà hàomǎ shì duōshao? 你的电话号码是多少?

tell someone your telephone number:
Wǒ de diànhuà hàomǎ shì sān-líng-èr-yāo-yāo-sì-qī. 我的电话号码是 3021147。

tell someone you will telephone them:
Wǒ míngtiān gěi nǐ dǎ (yí gè) diànhuà. 我明天给你打(一个)电话。

ask to speak to someone on the telephone:
Qǐng Ānnà jiē diànhuà, hǎo mà? 请安娜接电话，好吗?

leave a message asking someone to ring you back:
Qǐng nín ràng tā gěi wǒ huí diànhuà. 请您让她给我回电话。

pass on a message about ringing someone back:
Tā ràng nǐ huí diànhuà. 他让你回电话。

Useful expressions
jiālǐ yǒu shìr 家里有事儿 *something on at home*
Zhèiyàng ba, ... 这样吧,...... *How about if ...? Let's do it this way, ...*
Yíhuìr huílai 一会儿回来 *be back soon*
Nǐ dǎcuò diànhuà le! 你打错电话了! *You've called the wrong number!*

学会写字 第一课 (Xuéhuì xiě zì Dì-yī kè) (1.1)

● 汉字表

dōu
all; both

tóng
same; together with

xǐ   *like; be fond of*

huān
joyfully

短文 ⊙⊙
duǎn

　老师好，同学们好！我叫王星，今年十三岁。我家有四个人，爸爸、妈妈、妹妹和我。我没有哥哥、姐姐和弟弟。我爸爸是老师，妈妈也是老师。我和妹妹都是中学生，在同一个学校上学。我们都很喜欢我们的学校。

学会写字 第二课 (Xuéhuì xiě zì   Dì-èr kè) (1.2)

● 汉字表

事	shì *affair; business*	儿	er *(retroflex ending)*	去	qù *to go; last (as in qùnián)*
玩	wán *to have fun; play*	来	lái *to come*		

对话

A: 小明,今天下午你
在家吗?

B: 在,什么事儿?

A: 我去你家玩儿,好
吗?

B: 好,你来吧。

学会写字 第三课 (Xuéhuì xiě zì   Dì-sān kè) (1.3)

● 汉字表

本	běn *(measure word); book*	看	kàn *look; watch; read*	说	shuō *to say*

借	jiè *borrow; lend*
行	xíng *OK; be all right*

对话 📟

A: 这本小说是谁的？

B: 是我的。

A: 好看吗？

B: 很好看。我很喜欢这本小说。

A: 借我看，好吗？

B: 行。

学会写字 第四课 (Xuéhuì xiě zì　Dì-sì kè) (1.4)

● 汉字表

了	le *(aspect particle indicating completion or change)*	正	zhèng *(aspect particle indicating action in progress)*	做	zuò *do, make*
作	zuò *do, act, compose, write*	业	yè *(as in zuòyè)*	多	duō *many, much*

对话 🆑

弟弟：几点了？

哥哥：十点了。

弟弟：十点了？这么晚！

哥哥：你正在做什么？

弟弟：做作业。

哥哥：做作业？今天你们的作业很多，是吗？

弟弟：不，这是上星期的作业。

学会写字 第五课 (Xuéhuì xiě zì Dì-wǔ kè)   (1.5)

● 汉字表

王	wáng *(a surname)* *king, prince*	打	dǎ *to strike; to play (ball games)*	球	qiú *ball*
得	de *(structural particle)* děi *must, have to*	真	zhēn *real, true; genuine*	更	gèng *even more; more*

对话 💿

A: 那是谁？

B: 王星的妹妹。

A: 她打球打得真好！王星和他的妹
妹，谁打得更好？

B: 王星。

C: 他们两个都打得很好。

学会写字 第六课 (Xuéhuì xiě zì   Dì-liù kè)   (1.6)

● 汉字表

	zhī to know		dào way, path road		diàn electricity; electric

话	huà (something said or written); words, talk; language

对话 💿

小明：王星在家吗？

妹妹：不在，他去学校了。

小明：他几点回来？

妹妹：不知道。

小明：我是他的同学小明。你叫他给
我回电话，好吗？

妹妹：好。

小明：我的电话是二五七一三九〇
四。

---

* The character 零 *ling* (meaning 'zero') is commonly written as 'O' in numbers.

UNIT 2

What shall I wear?

第二单元

Dì-èr   dānyuán

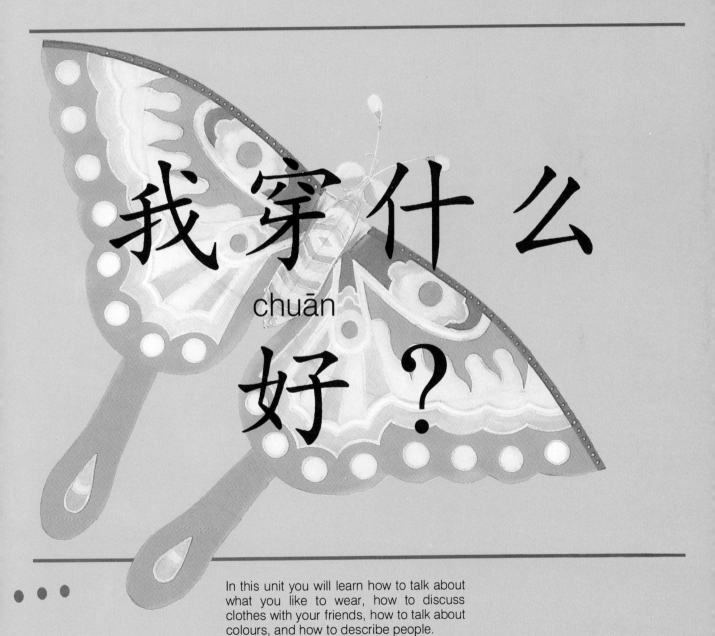

我 穿 什 么

chuān

好 ？

In this unit you will learn how to talk about what you like to wear, how to discuss clothes with your friends, how to talk about colours, and how to describe people.

2.1   What are they wearing?

China is a country of many nationalities. Each nationality has its own national dress, many of which are very exotic and colourful.

The dress that is perhaps most identified as being Chinese is the close-fitting *qípáo* (旗袍) or 'cheongsam' for women, which is characterised by a one-piece front buttoned to the right side, a high collar and slits along the sides of the skirt.

Traditionally, men wore a long gown called a *dàguà* (大褂)，but this has long been superseded by the Chinese-style jacket and the *Zhōngshān zhuāng* (中山装)。Today more and more people tend to wear Western-style clothes.

他穿什么? 🔊

(Tā chuān shénme?)

Nowadays, people tend to dress fairly simply in the kind of clothing you see in these pictures.

1.

兰兰 穿 衬衫 和 牛仔裤。
lánlán chuān chènshān niúzǎikù

2.

冬冬 穿 汗衫 和 短裤。
dōngdōng chuān hànshān duǎnkù

3.

小云 穿 运动服，
yún chuān fú

袜子 和 球鞋。
wàzi xié

4.

建华 戴 帽子 和 墨镜。
jiànhuá dài màozi mòjìng

他 没有 穿 鞋。
chuān xié

长裤
chángkù

Wearing things 🔊

Note that in Chinese there are two different ways of saying 'wear': 穿 *chuān*, which is used for items of clothing and shoes, and 戴 *dài*, which is used for 'accessories'. Here are some things you would 穿 and some you would 戴 with their measure words.

我穿……
衣服 yīfu *clothes* (件 jiàn)
衬衫 chènshān *shirt*
汗衫 hànshān *T-shirt*
毛衣 máoyī *jumper*
外套 wàitào *jacket*
裙子 qúnzi *skirt* (条 tiáo)
短裤 duǎnkù *shorts*
西装 xīzhuāng *suit* (套 tào)
袜子 wàzi *socks* (双 shuāng 只 zhī)
球鞋 qiúxié *sneakers*

我戴……
帽子 màozi *hat, cap* (顶 dǐng)
墨镜(儿) mòjìng(r) *sunglasses* (副 fù)
领带 lǐngdài *tie* (条 tiáo)
(手)表 (shǒu)biǎo *(wrist)watch* (块 kuài)

What are the English equivalents of the measure words 件，条，套，双，顶，副，块 and 只?

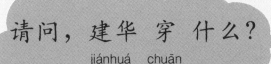

请问，建华 穿 什么?
jiánhuá chuān

● 该 你 了！ (Gāi nǐ le!)

西装（套）
xīzhuāng tào

裙子（条）
qúnzi tiáo

毛衣（件）
máoyī jiàn

领带（条）
lǐngdài tiáo

外套（件）
wàitào jiàn

张 老师 今天 穿 什么 衣服？
zhāng   chuān   yīfu

丁 老师 今天 穿 什么 衣服？
dīng   chuān   yīfu

王 勇 呢？
    yǒng

● 穿 上 外 套！ (Chuānshàng wàitào!)

妈妈：你 穿 得 太 少 了！
        chuān

今天 天气 很 冷，
你 出去 要 多 穿 点儿 衣服。
    chū   chuān   yīfu

你有什么衣服？

More items of clothing and accessories — which ones do you own?

校服 xiàofú *school uniform*
上衣 shàngyī *coat*
背心 bèixīn *singlet*
毛背心 máobèixīn
    sleeveless woollen sweater
连衣裙 liányīqún *dress*
连衣裤 liányīkù *jumpsuit*
短裙 duǎnqún *short skirt*
超短裙 chāoduǎnqún
    mini-skirt
甲克 jiǎkè *jacket*
皮甲克 pí jiǎkè *leather jacket*
健身衣 jiànshēnyī *bodysuit;*
    leotards
大衣 dàyī *coat; overcoat*
短大衣 duǎndàyī *short coat*
睡衣 shuìyī *pyjamas*
游泳裤 yóuyǒngkù
    swimming togs
游泳衣 yóuyǒngyī *swimsuit*
三点式泳衣 sāndiǎnshì yǒngyī
    bikini (swimwear)

长筒袜 chángtǒngwà
    stockings
裤袜 kùwà *pantyhose*
皮鞋 píxié *leather shoes*
高跟鞋 gāogēnxié
    high-heeled shoes
平底鞋 píngdǐxié *flat-heeled*
    shoes
长筒鞋 chángtǒngxié *boots*
便鞋 biànxié *casual shoes*
拖鞋 tuōxié *slippers, thongs*
凉鞋 liángxié *sandals*

头盔 tóukuī *helmet*
围巾 wéijīn *scarf*
手套 shǒutào *gloves*
眼镜(儿) yǎnjìng(r) *glasses*
耳环 ěrhuán *earring*
手表 shǒubiǎo *watch*
手镯 shǒuzhuó *bracelet*
戒指 jièzhi *ring*

小明： 好。……

我 走 了。

妈妈： 你 要 走 了？

不行，你 穿 得 还 不 够，
　　　　　chuān　　　　　gòu

穿 外套 去！
chuān　wàitào

小明： 不用 了，我 穿 了 一 件 毛衣。
　　　　　chuān　　　jiàn　máoyī

妈妈： 一 件 毛衣 怎么 够 呢？
　　　jiàn　máoyī　　　gòu

现在 刮 大 风，很 冷 啊！
　　　guā　　fēng

穿上 这 件 外套！
chuān　　jiàn　wàitào

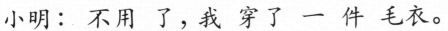

小明： 那 好 吧。

穿 衣服　戴　摘
chuān　fú

Find the Chinese

It's extremely windy.
That won't do.
I'm off now.
Put on this jacket!
All right then.
You still aren't wearing enough.
If you're going out you should put on plenty of clothes.
Go and put on a jacket.
You're going now?
There's no need.
I've put on a jumper.

怎么说?

1. Mum tells Xiao Ming to put on a coat by saying

    "穿上这件外套"

    How would you tell someone to put on the following?
    a) these shoes
    b) these sunglasses
    c) these socks
    d) this hat
    e) this tie
    f) this jumper

2. If you were advising someone to dress more warmly, you might say to them:

    "你要多穿(点儿)衣服"

    How would you advise someone to do the following?
    a) watch more movies
    b) play less table tennis
    c) return home quickly
    d) quickly come and look

Notes:

1. *Chuān wàitào qù!* — This is another, more emphatic way of saying *Qù chuān wàitào!*

2. *Nǐ chūqu yào duō chuān diǎnr yīfu* — The adjective *duō* (多) may be used to qualify a verb, as in *duō chuān* (多穿). *Shǎo* (少), *kuài* (快), *màn* (慢) may also be used in this way. For example:

    Shǎo kàn diànshì. Watch less television.
    Kuài lái ya! Come here, quickly!
    Nín màn zǒu. Zàijiàn! Goodbye! Take care.

3. *Nǐ chūqu yào duō chuān diǎnr yīfu* — *Yào* (要) can also mean 'need to', 'must' or 'should'. This use of *yào* is negated by *bú yào* (should not) or *búyòng* (不用 need not). (Also see box on page 48.)

The box below summarises the different uses of 要 you have learnt so far.

Indicating	Example	Negative form
intention	我要看电视。 *I intend to watch television.*	我不想看电视。 *I do not intend to watch television.*
that one should or ought to ...	你要穿大衣。 *You should wear a coat.*	你不用穿大衣。 *You needn't wear a coat.*

Find the Chinese → page 47
怎么说? → page 47
你跳舞穿什么衣服? →
穿上衣服 →

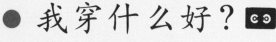

● 我穿什么好? 📼
(Wǒ chuān shénme hǎo?)

1. 建华 今天 要 去 安娜 家 吃 晚饭。
jiànhuá   ānnà

你 觉得 他 穿 什么 好?
jué   chuān

我 觉得 他 最 好 是
jué

穿 长裤 和 皮鞋。
chuān chángkù   píxié

你跳舞穿什么衣服?

Work in pairs. Take turns to ask each other about what clothes, shoes, and so on you wear to go:
- dancing
- to school
- shopping
- bike riding
- visiting friends
- playing tennis
- jogging
- to do aerobics

穿上衣服!
Put some clothes on!

Work in pairs.

1. Each draw a stick figure. One of you clothe your stick figure by drawing items of clothing on it. As you do this, tell your partner what your stick figure is wearing so that your partner can clothe his or her stick figure in exactly the same way. Your partner does not look at your sketch but listens to what you are saying. When you have both finished drawing clothes on your stick figures, compare your drawings. Are your stick figures wearing the same items of clothing?

   Now change over. Remember to speak only Chinese throughout this activity!

2. Cut out three figures from clothing advertisements. You and your partner each secretly choose one. Then find out which one your partner has chosen by asking questions.

2.

玛丽 想 去 海边儿。
mǎlì　　　　hǎibiānr

你 觉得 她 穿 什么 好?
　jué　　　　chuān

3. 大卫 想 骑 自行车 去 玩儿。
　wèi　　qí　　　　　　wánr

你 觉得 他 穿 什么 好?
　jué　　　　chuān

我 不 知道 穿 什么 好!
　　　　　chuān

LEARN TO READ　page 65

LEARN TO WRITE　Lesson 7　page 73

2.2 How does it look?

● 你觉得怎么样？

(Nǐ juéde zěnmeyàng?)

1.

怎么样？

这 双 鞋 有 点儿 紧。
shuāng xié jǐn

2.

你 看 我 穿 这 件 衣服
chuān jiàn yīfu
怎么样？

你 最 好 是
穿 得 漂亮 一点儿！
chuān piàoliàng

3.

这样 好看 吗？

我 觉得 你 戴 领带
jué dài lǐng
更 好看。

4.

这 顶 帽子 合适 吗？
dǐng màozi héshì

我 觉得 样子 挺 怪 的。
jué zi guài

5.

你 觉得 这 条 裙子
jué   tiáo   qúnzi

怎么 样？

挺 新潮 的。我 喜欢！
   xīncháo

6.

这 件 衣服 挺 合身 的，
jiàn   yīfu   héshēn

你 看 呢？

太 肥 了！我 不 喜欢！
   féi

7.

你 喜欢 我 的 新鞋 吗？
          xīn xié

样子 不 够 时髦。
zi   gòu   máo

Here are more words you can use to describe clothes: 📼

难看 nánkàn *ugly*
一般 yìbān *ordinary*
舒服 shūfu *comfortable*
长 cháng *long*
短 duǎn *short*
大 dà *big*
小 xiǎo *small*
复杂 fùzá *complicated; fussy*
花 huā *flowery; gaudy*

我 的 新衣服 怎么
       xīn
样？

Work in pairs. Cut out eight items of clothing from a magazine or advertisement. Shuffle the cutouts then deal out four each. Take it in turns to ask your partner's opinion on your 'new' (xīn) shoes, hat, tracksuit or whatever is in your cut-outs. For example, you could ask:

你 看 我 的 新甲克 怎
         xīn jiǎkè
么样？

You can report to the class:

xx 说 我 的 ……，

and ask other students their opinion. For example:

你 看 呢？

Notes:

Nǐ kàn ne? — 'What do you think?' This is another way of asking someone's opinion. When expressing your opinion, you can say

'*Wǒ kàn . . .*'. For example: *Wǒ kàn zhè tiáo kùzi tài dà le!*

我 的 新 衣服 怎么样？ →

● 该你了! (Gāi nǐ le!)

What do you think the people in the drawings think about these clothes?
Match the comments to the pictures.

A. 那 条 裙子 不 够 ……!
     tiáo qún   gòu

B. 那 顶 帽子 ……!
     dǐng mào

C. 这 件 睡衣 太 …… 了!
     jiàn

D. 这 双 鞋 ……!
     shuāng xié

E. 那 条 裤子 样子 ……。
     tiáo

F. 这 件 衬衫 ……。
     jiàn chènshān

G. 这 条 ……。
     tiáo

● 说汉语 (一) 🔊

海伦: 喂，安娜! …… 你 好!
hǎilún wèi ānnà

安娜: 好 久 不 见 了，
ānnà   jiǔ

     怎么样? 好 吗?

海伦: 挺 好 的。
hǎilún

安娜: 你 也 来 买 东西 啊?
ānnà   mǎi dōngxi

海伦: 不，随便 看看。你 呢?
hǎilún   suíbiàn

安娜：我 想 买 一 条 牛仔裤。
ānnà　　　　mǎi　tiáo　niúzǎikù

服务员：你 觉得 这 条 怎么样?
fúwùyuán　　jué　tiáo

海伦：挺 时髦 的。
　　　　　máo

安娜：我 觉得 太 时髦 了!
　　　jué　　máo

服务员：这 条 呢?
fúwùyuán　tiáo

安娜：这 条 不错。
　　　tiáo　cuò

海伦：样子 还 可以。你 试试 看。
　　　zi　　　　　　shìshì

服务员：挺 合身 的。
fúwùyuán　héshēn

海伦：我 觉得 有 点儿 短。
　　　　jué　　　duǎn

安娜：哦,是 有 点儿 短。
　　　ò　　　　duǎn

(to shop assistant)

有 长 一点儿 的 吗?
　cháng

服务员：有,请 等 一 等,我 去 拿。
fúwùyuán　　děng　děng

Notes:

1. *Ò, shì yǒu diǎnr duǎn — Shì* (是) is used here for emphasis and is stressed when uttered.

2. *Yǒu cháng yìdiǎnr de ma? — Cháng yìdiǎnr de* (a bit longer) refers to the pair of trousers. This is understood from the context. Note that an 'adjective + *de* (的)' construction (*cháng de* 长的) can stand by itself as a noun so that it represents whatever is being described. This structure is similar to the 'noun + (*de* 的)' construction you learned in *Hànyǔ for Beginning Students* when referring to something (for example, a book or a pet) belonging to a friend:

    Zhè bú shì wǒ de, shì wǒ péngyou de.

Find the Chinese →
怎么说? →

我在等你呢!

(Wǒ zài děng nǐ ne!)

Find the Chinese

They fit well.
Yes, they *are* a bit short.
What do you think of this pair?
I'll try them on.
I want to buy a pair of jeans.
I'm just looking.
Do you have any that are a bit longer?
The style's OK.
I'll get you a longer pair.
Haven't seen you for ages.
Are you doing some shopping too?
I think they are a bit *too* trendy!

怎么说?

1. How did Anna ask Helen if she had come to do some shopping?
    How would you ask someone if they have come to do the following?
    a) play tennis
    b) see a movie
    c) listen to music
    d) wait for a friend

2. How did Anna ask the shop assistant for a longer pair of jeans? If you were shopping for jeans, how would you ask for the following?
    a) a shorter pair
    b) a more fashionable pair
    c) a tighter pair
    d) a looser pair
    e) a smaller pair
    f) a bigger pair

LEARN TO READ   page 66

LEARN TO WRITE   Lesson 8   page 74

2.3 What colour is it?

● 这是什么颜色？ 📼
(Zhè shì shénme yánsè?)

黑（色）
hēi sè

白（色）
bái sè

灰（色）
huī sè

棕（色）
zōng sè

黄（色）
huáng sè

蓝（色）
lán sè

绿（色）
lǜ sè

紫（色）
zǐ sè

红（色）
hóng sè

橙（色）
chéng sè

浅 蓝色
qiǎn   lánsè

深 蓝色
shēn   lánsè

我 喜欢 绿色。
lǜsè

我 最 喜欢 蓝色 了!
lánsè

请问，你 喜欢 什么 颜色？
yánsè

Colours

As in other cultures, certain colours have special significance for the Chinese. Red is the traditional colour of joy and happiness and the colour red predominates at festive occasions such as weddings or Spring Festival. Yellow and gold traditionally signify heavenly glory and these colours, together with red, are the dominant colours in imperial buildings and temples. Blue is the colour of heaven and is seen to represent meditation and tranquility. It is also often associated with the common people. Black is seen as representing disaster, grief and evil. White signifies purity and is also the colour of mourning for the Chinese.

Notes:

The colours *hēi*, *bái*, *huī*, *zōng*, *huáng*, *lán* and so on are all adjectives. *Sè* (色) is a noun meaning 'colour'. So when you place *sè* (色) after a colour (for example, *hēisè* 黑色, *báisè* 白色), it literally means 'the colour black', 'the colour white' and so on.

● 颜色好看不好看？

(Yánsè hǎokàn bù hǎokàn?)

我 喜欢 穿 灰 衬衫，
　　　　　　huī　chènshān
蓝 裤子。你 觉得 怎么样？
lán

你 穿 灰 衬衫、蓝 裤子，
　　　huī　chènshān　lán
应该 配 黑色 的 皮鞋。
yīnggāi　pèi　hēi　　　píxié

这条 裤子 好看 不 好看？
颜色 不 好看。
yánsè

我 觉得 那 条 绿 的
　　　　　　　　lǜ
更 好看。

我 穿 这件 衬衫
　　　　　chènshān
好看 不 好看？

挺 好 的，可是，我 觉得
你 穿 蓝 衬衫 最 好看！
lán　chènshān

Notes:

1. *Huī chènshān, lán kùzi* — A single-syllable adjective may be placed immediately in front of a noun to describe it. However, this is governed to a large extent by usage.
2. *Yīnggāi chuān hēisè de píxié* — When a noun (*hēisè*) is used to describe another noun, *de* (的) is generally placed between them to indicate this relationship.

Find the Chinese →
怎么说? →

Here's how you use colours to describe something. For example, *wàitào* and *máoyī*;

hēi bái huī huáng lán lǜ zǐ hóng	wàitào

If you use *sè* (色) with the colour, turning it into a noun, you must also use *de* (的). For example:

Hóng wàitào (红外套), but *hóngsè de wàitào* (红色的外套)

(Both of these examples mean 'a red jacket'.)

hēisè báisè huīsè zōngsè huángsè lánsè lǜsè zǐsè hóngsè shēn lánsè qiǎn huīsè	**de** máoyī

Find the Chinese

I think the green ones are better.
You should wear black shoes with them.
I think if you wore a blue shirt it would look best of all.
Do you think these slacks look good?
How would this shirt look on me?

怎么说?

How does the girl say that she thinks the green pair looks better?
How would you tell a friend that you think the following?

- the blue ones look better
- the red ones are more fashionable
- the black ones are uglier
- the yellow ones would be more comfortable

More colours

橙色	chéngsè	*orange*
浅蓝色	qiǎn lánsè	*light blue*
深灰色	shēn huīsè	*dark grey*
粉红色	fěnhóngsè	*pink*
银灰色	yínhuīsè	*silver grey*
金色	jīnsè	*gold*
米黄色	mǐhuángsè	*beige*
咖啡色	kāfēisè	*light brown*
草绿色	cǎolǜsè	*grass green*

● 你的球鞋是什么颜色的？ 🔊

(Nǐ de qiúxié shì shénme yánsè de?)

Here's how you can ask what colour something is:

Nǐ de qiúxié	shì	shénme yánsè	de?
Wǒ de qiúxié	shì	hóng huáng lán báisè lǜsè	de.

请问，他的衣服是什么颜色的？ →
'Come as you are' party! →

● 说汉语（二）🔊

海伦：参加 小明 的 生日会，
hǎilún   cānjiā

你 说，我 穿 这 件 衬衫 好
                              chènshān

还是 穿 那 件 衬衫 好？
            chènshān

托尼：你 穿 什么 裤子？
tuōní

海伦：这 条。
hǎilún

托尼：我 觉得 这 两 件 衬衫 跟
tuōní   chènshān

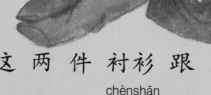

这 条 牛仔裤 都 挺 不 配 的。
        niú zǎi   pèi

请问，他的衣服是什么颜色的？

Form teams of four or five persons each. Each team prepares a colour picture or a collage of a group of people. Tag each person in the picture with a name.

Display the picture for one minute to your rival group, then hide it. Ask your rival team to recall what each person is wearing and the colour of his or her clothes. Keep score of correct and incorrect answers.

A traced outline of the picture with the name of each individual may be shown to help in identifying who's who in your picture.

'Come as you are' party!

You can hold this party in two ways:

1. Everyone writes or sketches five different items of clothing on slips of paper according to five categories: tops, bottoms, head-gear, footwear, miscellaneous. All the slips are put in their categories, then scrambled. Each person then draws out one slip from each pile. This will be what that person wears to the party! When you have your party outfit, sketch and label it, then display your sketch on the wall.

2. Work in small groups where different people take turns to nominate a particular time. For example:

"上星期六下午六点"

Everyone writes down or sketches what they were wearing at that particular time. Then members of the group take turns to describe what they were wearing while the rest of the group make sketches according to the description. Finally, everyone compares their sketches.

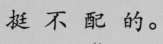

那 件 浅 蓝色 的 衬衫 挺
　　　qiǎn　lánsè　　　chènshān

好 的。你 怎么 不 穿 呢?

海伦: 那 件 我 穿 起来 有 点儿
hǎilún

紧。
jǐn

托尼: 你 还 有 一 件 红 衬衫 吧?
tuōní　　　　　　　　　　hóng　chènshān

海伦: 那 件⋯⋯。
hǎilún

托尼: 我 觉得 红 衬衫 跟 这 条
tuōní　　　　　hóng　chènshān

牛仔裤 挺 配 的。
niú zǎi　pèi

海伦: 是 吗?
托尼: 你 试 一 试。
　　　shì　　shì

海伦: 好。
托尼: 挺 好看 的,
　　　你 说 呢?
海伦: 对, 我 也
　　　觉得 不错。
　　　　　　cuò

Find the Chinese

I think it looks good too.
That one's a bit tight on me.
Your pale blue shirt would look good.
You've also got a red shirt, haven't you?
What do you think?
What pants are you wearing?
Do you think I should I wear this shirt or that one to Xiao Ming's birthday party?
A red shirt would go well with these jeans.
Is that so?
I don't think either of these shirts goes with those jeans.

怎么说?

How did Helen say that her light blue shirt was a bit tight on her? How would she tell someone that it was:

- a bit loose?
- a bit short?
- a bit long?

你听懂了吗?

True or false?

1. a) The boy is going to a movie.
   b) He is going to take Anna out to dinner.
   c) Anna is taking him out to dinner.

2. a) The girl takes colour and style into consideration when choosing clothes.
   b) She doesn't care about style as long as the colour is OK.
   c) She doesn't consider colour as long as the clothes are stylish.

3. When the boy finally got dressed, he was wearing:
   a) a grey tie
   b) a red tie
   c) a green tie

Find the Chinese →
怎么说? →
你听懂了吗? →

LEARN TO READ page 67
LEARN TO WRITE
Lesson 9 page 75

2.4 Describing people

● 她长得什么样儿？ 📼

(Tā zhǎng de shénme yàngr?)

眼睛
yǎnjing

脸
liǎn

鼻子
bízi

头发
tóufa

耳朵
ěrduo

嘴巴
zuǐba

1.

林 青 长 得 什么 样儿？
　　qīng　zhǎng

她 长 得 挺 胖 的。
　zhǎng　　　　pàng

她 的 脸 是 圆 的。
　　　liǎn　　yuán

她 的 眼睛 是 黑 的。
　　　yǎnjing　hēi

她 的 嘴巴 很 小。
　　　zuǐba

她 的 皮肤 挺 白 的。
　　　pífū

2. 陈 先生 长 得 什么 样儿?
   chén xiān   zhǎng

他 戴 眼镜。
dài   yǎnjìng

他 有 胡子。
          hú

他 的 鼻子 挺 大 的。
      bí

他 的 耳朵 也 挺 大 的。
      ěrduo

他 的 头发 很 长。
      tóufa

他 个子 很 高。
          gāo

Here are some more descriptions you may want to use when describing someone. 📻

Eyes
她的眼睛是蓝的。(blue)
  绿的 (green)
  棕色的 (brown)

Face
他的脸 (liǎn) 挺长的。(long)

Hair
他的头发很短。* (short)
她的头发是直 (zhí) 的。
  (straight)
  卷 (juǎn) 的 (curly)
  金 (jīn) 色的 (blond,
    blonde)
  黄色的 (blond, blonde)
  红色的 (red)
  黑色的 (black)
  棕色的 (brown)
他是光头 (guāngtóu)。(bald)

Complexion
她的皮肤 (pífū) 挺黑的。(dark)

Height
她个子 (gèzi) 很矮。* (short)

Build
她挺瘦的。(thin)

* Note that duǎn (短) is used when referring to length and ǎi (矮) when referring to height.

3. 你 看 这 孩子 长 得 真 漂亮!
   hái   zhǎng   piàoliang

是 啊, 他 真 好玩儿!

Notes:

Tā zhǎng de shénme yàngr? — *Yàngr* (样儿) means 'appearance' or 'shape' and is the same as *yàngzi* (样子).

Wanted 🔘

The police are after a robber. Here is a description given by a witness.
Which of the four suspects is she describing?

他 很 胖。他 的 头发 很 长，眼睛
　　　pàng　　　　　　tóufa　　　　　　　yǎnjing

很 小。他 的 嘴巴 很 大，鼻子 也
　　　　　　　　zuǐba　　　　　　bí

很 大。

它们真奇怪！ 🔘 (Tāmen zhēn qíguài!)

Can you describe each of these animals?
You might want to use some of these words:

头 *tóu* head
脖子 *bózi* neck
胳膊 *gēbo* arm
手 *shǒu* hand
肚子 *dùzi* belly
腿 *tuǐ* leg
脚 *jiǎo* foot
尾巴 *wěiba* tail
毛 *máo* hair; fur

猴子
hóuzi

二十只青蛙 →

二十只青蛙 🔘
(Èrshí zhī qīngwā)

一只青蛙，
　一个鼻子，
　两只眼睛，
　四条腿。

"扑通！" (pūtōng)
　跳下水。

One frog,
　One nose,
　Two eyes,
　Four legs,
　'Splash!'
Into the water it jumps.

Reword the verse for 2, 3, 4,
5, . . . up to 20 frogs. Remember
that each frog makes its own
splash!

● 真奇怪！ 🔘 (Zhēn qíguài!)

1. A: 对不起，现在 几 点 了？

   B: 六 点 一 刻。
   　　　　　　　kè

   A: 我 的 表 也 是 六 点 一 刻。真 奇 怪！
   　　　　　　　　　　　　　　　kè　　　　　qíguài

B: 怎么 啦？

A: 我 正在 等 人。
　　　　　　děng

B: 是 男 的 还是 女 的？
　　　nán　　　　　nǚ

A: 是 女 的。是 一 个 女 孩子。
　　　nǚ　　　　　　　　nǚ hái

B: 她 长 得 什么 样儿？
　　　zhǎng

A: 她 戴 眼镜，个子 挺 高 的，
　　dài yǎnjìng　　　　　gāo

不 胖 不 瘦，头发 很 长。
pàng　　shòu tóufa

2. B: 她 的 头发 是 金色 的 吗？
　　　　　tóufa　　jīnsè

A: 是，是！

B: 她 头发 挺 长 的？

A: 是！她 在 哪儿，您 知道 吗？
　　　　　　　　　nín

B: 那 是 不 是 她？

A: 是，是 她，是 她！谢谢！

B: 不用 谢。

3. A: 琳达！琳达！
　　　líndá

A: 哦，……对不起！
ò

C: 没 关系。
guānxi

4. D: 阿伦！
ālún

A: 琳达！你 来 啦！你 怎么 晚 了？！
líndá

D: 我 没有 晚 啊，你 说 我们
六 点 半 见面！
miàn

A: 哦，是 吗？对不起！对不起！
ò

我 以为 是 六 点！
wéi

Notes:
Shì nán de háishi nǔ de? — *Nán de* (男的) means 'male person', and *nǔ de* (女的) means 'female person'. *Nán* and *nǔ* are generally not used by themselves (i.e. we do not say *Tā shì nán, tā shì nǔ*) but in combination with some other word. For example:

nán háizi   *nǔ háizi*
nán tóngxué   *nǔ tóngxué*
nán lǎoshī   *nǔ lǎoshī*
nán xuésheng (nánshēng)   *nǔ xuésheng (nǔshēng)*
Wǒmen de lǎoshī shì nán de.   *Nèi gè nǔ de shì shéi?*

Find the Chinese →
他(她)是谁? →

LEARN TO READ   page 69

LEARN TO WRITE   Lesson 10   page 76

Find the Chinese

Is that her?
I'm not late.
What's the matter?
I thought it was 6!
You're here!
What does she look like?
Male or female?
She's rather tall.
How come you're late?
You said we'd meet at 6.30.
That's strange!

他(她)是谁?

Think of someone known to the class. Jot down his or her name. Describe that person to your classmate who has to figure out who that person is. You could describe a member of the class or a teacher. You can describe age, height, build, hair colour, whether he or she wears glasses or not and so on.

学会认字 (Xuéhuì rèn zì)

2.1

Before reading the text, listen to the recording and answer the questions.

True or false?
1. The dialogue is about Mum refusing to allow her son to go and see his friend.
2. The son was wearing a pair of trousers.
3. It was a cold day.
4. They were looking for something in the house.
5. In the end the son did not go out.

● 汉字表

				As in
哪	nǎ	which; what		哪儿
穿	chuān	to wear		穿衣服
衣	yī	clothing		衣服
服	fú	clothes		
长	cháng	long		长裤
裤	kù	trousers		
出	chū	go out, come out		出去

Text

妈妈： 你要去哪儿?

弟弟： 我要去朋友家。

妈妈： 今天天气很冷,
多穿点儿衣服。

弟弟： 我穿了不少了!

妈妈： 不行! 今天很冷,
你得穿长裤出去。

弟弟： 我不怕冷！

妈妈： 不行！穿长裤去！

弟弟： 我的长裤在哪儿？

妈妈： 你找一找。

        我也帮你找。

        ……

动动脑筋

(Dòngdong nǎojīn)

1. Do you know how to do this?

    做衣服

2. Who in your class would wear a

    游泳衣？

2.2

Before reading the text, listen to the recording and answer the questions.

True or false?
1. The speakers are in a shop.
2. They had arranged to meet there before coming.
3. They chose exactly the same item.
4. They both decided to buy something.

● 汉字表

			As in
久	jiǔ	for a long time	好久不见
买	mǎi	to buy	买东西
东	dōng	east	东西
西	xī	west	
呀	ya	(=啊 after a, e, i, o, ü)	买东西呀？
条	tiáo	(measure word)	一条长裤
短	duǎn	short	短裤
子	zi	(noun suffix)	样子
觉	jué	to feel	觉得

动动脑筋

(Dòngdong nǎojīn)

1. The two people in the dialogue use the terms 小号, 中号 when they discuss the clothes they want to buy.
    What do you think they mean?
    What do you think

    大号

    would mean?

Text 🔊   好长时间   好多长时间

A: 好久不见了！怎么样？好吗？

    Tìng hǎo de

B: 挺好的，你呢？

A: 也挺好的。

你来买东西呀？

B: 是，我想买条短裤。

你说这条短裤样子好看不好看？

A: 我觉得挺好看的。

我很喜欢。

B: 我也觉得好看。

好，我买一条。

A: 我也想买一条。

B: 好啊，你也买一条吧。

A: 好，你穿几号？

B: 我穿小号。

A: 我穿中号。

2. A pair of trousers is said to be

不长不短。

This means that it will be:
a) not very short
b) just right
c) too long

3. If the compound 大小 means 'size', what do you think

长短

means?

4. Someone described as

说一不二

is someone who
a) can't make up his or her mind?
b) mispronounced the word 'one' for 'two'?
c) stands by his or her word?

2.3

Before reading the text, listen to the recording and answer the questions.

True or false?
1. The two girls are sisters.
2. They were invited out to dinner.
3. They were discussing what they would wear.
4. The younger sister was going to wear a yellow shirt and a skirt.
5. The shirt belonged to her elder sister.

● 汉字表

			As in
件	jiàn	(measure word)	三件衣服
红	hóng	red	红裤子
衬	chèn	lining	衬衫
衫	shān	unlined upper garment	
白	bái	white	白衬衫
配	pèi	to match	白衬衫配红裤子

黄	huáng	*yellow*	黄衬衫
试	shì	*to try*	试衣服；试试看
合	hé	*to suit*	合身
身	shēn	*body*	
双	shuāng	*(measure word) pair*	这双黑鞋
黑	hēi	*black*	黑裤子；一双黑鞋
鞋	xié	*shoe*	黑鞋；球鞋

Text

1. 妹妹：姐姐，星期五晚上，
谢汉生请我吃饭。
你说，我穿什么好？

　　姐姐：穿你那件红衬衫吧。
你穿那件红衬衫挺好看的。

　　妹妹：我那件红衬衫穿起来
有点儿小。

　　姐姐：是吗？
那你穿这件白衬衫。

　　妹妹：这件白衬衫跟这条裤子配
吗？

　　姐姐：不太配。

2. 姐姐：对了，我有一件黄衬衫，
样子挺好看。
你穿穿看。

　　妹妹：你的衣服我穿起来
有点儿大吧？

　　姐姐：不大。你试试看。
……

动动脑筋

(Dòngdong nǎojīn)

1. Do you know anyone who can be described as a

   a) 白人？
   b) 黑人？

2. When during the day does this refer to?

   白天

3. Do you know of any siblings who may be described as

   双生？

挺合身的！

妹妹：　那我就穿你这件黄衬衫
　　　　跟这条裤子；配上这双黑鞋，
　　　　你看怎么样？

姐姐：　很好看，
　　　　星期五你就穿这一身儿！

2.4

Before reading the text, listen to the recording and answer the questions.

<u>Dialogue 1</u>

True or false?

1.　The girl and boy were trying to determine what someone else was wearing.
2.　The person they were referring to was tall.
3.　The girl wanted to know whether the girl in a black skirt was Xiao Ming's girlfriend.

<u>Dialogue 2</u>

True or false?

1.　The boy was with his little brother.
2.　The girls had never met the little boy before.
3.　The little boy was tall for his age.
4.　The little boy was 3 years old.
5.　He had large eyes but was rather skinny.

<u>Dialogue 3</u>

True or false?

1.　The girl knew that the boy had a pet dog.
2.　The girl had a pet dog just like the boy's.
3.　The girl loves animals.

● 汉字表

			As in
女	nǚ	woman; female	女的
高	gāo	tall; high	个子很高
头	tóu	head	头发
发	fà	hair	
裙	qún	skirt	裙子

孩	hái	*child*	孩子；小孩儿
玩	wán	*to have fun; play*	好玩儿
眼	yǎn	*eye*	眼睛
睛	jīng	*eyeball*	
胖	pàng	*fat; plump*	挺胖的
为	wéi	*to be, mean*	以为
漂	piào	*as in* piàoliang	漂亮
亮	liàng	*bright*	
狮	shī	*lion*	狮子狗

Text 🔊

1. a) G: 你知道那个女的是谁吗？

   B: 哪个女的？

   G: 在那儿呢，高个子，长头发。

   B: 是不是穿白裙子那个女的？

   G: 不是，是穿黑裙子的那个。

   B: 她呀，她是小明的女朋友。

2. G1: 这个小孩儿是你弟弟吗？

   B: 不是，是我姐姐的孩子。

   G1: 他真好玩儿！

   G2: 是啊，大眼睛，胖胖的，
       真好玩儿！
       他几岁了？

   B: 两岁。

   G1: 两岁？
       我以为他三岁了呢！

B: 是，他个子挺高的。

3. G: 这是谁的狗？
真漂亮！

B: 是我的。

G: 这是什么狗？

B: 这是小狮子狗*。

G: 真好看，我真喜欢！

动动脑筋

(Dòngdong nǎojīn)

1. Can you name the person in your school who could be described as the

   头头 (tóutou)?

2. What are you doing when this happens?

   天亮

---

* 狮子狗 (shīzigǒu) is a breed of small dog known as the Pekinese.
Shīzi means 'lion'.

SUMMARY

(LTR stands for Learn to Read; LTW stands for Learn to Write)

2.1 What are they wearing?

Now you can:

describe what someone is wearing or not wearing:
Dōngdōng chuān hànshān hé duǎnkù.
冬冬穿汗衫和短裤。
Jiànhuá dài màozi hé mòjìng.
建华戴帽子和墨镜。
Tā méiyǒu chuān xié. 他没有穿鞋。

ask someone's opinion about what to wear:
Nǐ juéde wǒ chuān shénme hǎo? 你觉得我穿什么好？

give advice about what to wear:
Wǒ juéde tā zuì hǎo shì chuān chángkù hé píxié.
我觉得他最好是穿长裤和皮鞋。
Nǐ chūqu yào duō chuān diǎnr yīfu.
你出去要多穿点儿衣服。

Useful expressions
Wǒ zǒu le. 我走了。 *I'm off now. Goodbye.*
Bù xíng. 不行。 *That won't do. It's not all right.*
Búyòng le. 不用了。 *There's no need.*
It's not necessary.

Nà hǎo ba. 那好吧。 *All right then.*
Màn zǒu. 慢走。 *Take care.*
(*said on saying goodbye*)

Extra vocabulary
more items of clothing　page 46

2.2 How does it look?

Now you can:

ask someone's opinion about clothes:
Nǐ juéde zhèi tiáo (kùzi) zěnmeyàng?
你觉得这条(裤子)怎么样？
Nǐ kàn wǒ chuān zhèi jiàn yīfu zěnmeyàng?
你看我穿这件衣服怎么样？

express your opinion about clothes:
Zhèi jiàn yīfu tǐng shímáo de.
这件衣服挺时髦的。
Zhèi jiàn yīfu yàngzi hái kěyǐ.
这件衣服样子还可以。
Wǒ juéde yàngzi tǐng guài de.
我觉得样子挺怪的。

say how well or otherwise clothes fit:
Zhèi jiàn yīfu tǐng héshēn de.
这件衣服挺合身的。
Zhèi shuāng xié yǒu diǎnr jǐn.
这双鞋有点儿紧。
Nǐ de kùzi tài féi le!   你的裤子太肥了!
Shì yǒu diǎnr duǎn.   是有点儿短。

give advice on how to dress:
Nǐ zuì hǎo shì chuān de piàoliang yìdiǎnr.
你最好是穿得漂亮一点儿。
Wǒ juéde nǐ dài lǐngdài gèng hǎokàn.
我觉得你戴领带更好看。

say you will try something on:
Wǒ shìshi kàn.   我试试看。

ask for something in a shop:
Wǒ kàn yíxià nèi shuāng xié, hǎo ma?
我看一下那双鞋, 好吗?
Yǒu cháng yìdiǎnr de ma?
有长一点儿的吗?

Useful expressions
Hǎo jiǔ bú jiàn le!   好久不见了!
   Haven't seen you for a long time!
Suíbiàn kànkan.   随便看看。 *Just looking.*
Nǐ kàn ne?   你看呢? *What do you think?*
   What's your view?
Nǐ kàn . . . ?   你看……? *Do you think . . . ?*
   In your opinion . . . ?

2.3   What colour is it?

Now you can:

describe the colour of someone's clothes:
huī chènshān, lán kùzi   灰衬衫、蓝裤子
hēisè de píxié   黑色的皮鞋
qiǎn lánsè de chènshān   浅蓝色的衬衫

ask someone's opinion about what to wear:
Nǐ shuō wǒ chuān zhèi jiàn chènshān hǎo háishi chuān
   nèi jiàn chènshān hǎo?   你说我穿这件衬衫好还是穿
   那件衬衫好?

give someone advice about what colour clothing to wear:
Wǒ juéde nèi tiáo lǜ de gèng hǎokàn.
   我觉得那条绿的更好看。
Wǒ juéde nǐ chuān lán chènshān zuì hǎokàn le!

我觉得你穿蓝衬衫最好看了!
Nǐ chuān huī chènshān, lán kùzi, yīnggāi pèi hēisè de
   píxié.   你穿灰衬衫、蓝裤子,应该配黑色的皮鞋。

say whether clothes go well together or not:
Wǒ juéde hóng chènshān gēn zhèi tiáo niúzǎikù tǐng pèi
   de.   我觉得红衬衫跟这条牛仔裤挺配的。
Zhèi liǎng jiàn chènshān gēn zhèi tiáo niúzǎikù dōu tǐng
   bú pèi de.   这两件衬衫跟这条牛仔裤都挺不配的。

Useful expressions
Nǐ shuō ne?   你说呢?   *What do you think?*
Shì ma?   是吗?   *Is that so? Do you think so?*

Extra vocabulary
more colours   page 57

2.4   Describing people

Now you can:

describe what somebody looks like:
Tā gèzi hěn ǎi.   他个子很矮。
Tā de tóufa hěn cháng.   他的头发很长。
Tā zhǎng de tǐng pàng de.   他长得挺胖的。
Tā yǒu húzi.   他有胡子。
Tā dài yǎnjìng.   她戴眼镜。
Tā shì nǚ de.   她是女的。

Useful expressions
Tā zhǎng de shénme yàngr?   他长得什么样儿?
   What does he look like?
Búyòng xiè.   不用谢。 *Don't mention it.*
   (response to thanks)

Extra vocabulary
more ways of describing people   page 61

学会写字 第七课 (Xuéhuì xiě zì   Dì-qī kè)   (2.1)

● 汉字表

要	yào to want; have to; need to	穿	chuān to wear	衣	yī clothing
服	fú clothes	少	shǎo few, less	太	tài extremely

对话

妈妈：你要去哪儿？

弟弟：我要去同学家。

妈妈：今天天气很冷，多穿点儿衣服。

弟弟：我穿得不少了！

妈妈：不行，你穿得太少了。

　　　穿上这个大衣！

学会写字 第八课 (Xuéhuì xiě zì   Dì-bā kè)   (2.2)

● 汉字表

影	yǐng *shadow*	件 jiàn *(measure word)*
长	cháng *long*	条 tiáo *(measure word)*
裤	kù *trousers*	

对话 🔊

A: 晚上我要去看电影。
   我穿这件上衣和这条长裤，
   好看不好看？
B: 我觉得这件上衣不好看。
A: 那件呢？
B: 那件好看。
A: 好，今天晚上我穿那件上衣和
   这条长裤。

学会写字 第九课 (Xuéhuì xiě zì   Dì-jiǔ kè) (2.3)

● 汉字表

Basic stroke

As in 乚 每

每	měi *each, every*	男	nán *male*	蓝	lán *blue*
灰	huī *grey*	子	zi *(suffix)*	女	nǚ *female*
白	bái *white*	裙	qún *skirt*		

对话 🔊

A: 你们每天上学要穿校服吗?

B: 要。

A: 你们穿什么校服?

B: 男生穿蓝上衣、灰裤子、女
生穿白上衣、蓝裙子。

学会写字 第十课 (Xuéhuì xiě zì Dì-shí kè) (2.4)

● 汉字表

孩	hái *child*	眼	yǎn *eye*	睛	jīng *eyeball*
胖	pàng *fat, plump*	高	gāo *tall, high*		

对话 🔊

A: 那个小男孩儿是谁的孩子？

B: 我姐姐的孩子。

A: 他真好玩儿！

C: 是啊，大眼睛，胖胖的，真好玩儿！

A: 他几岁了？

B: 两岁。

C: 两岁？他个子真高！

UNIT 3

Where's my book?

第三单元
Dì-sān dānyuán

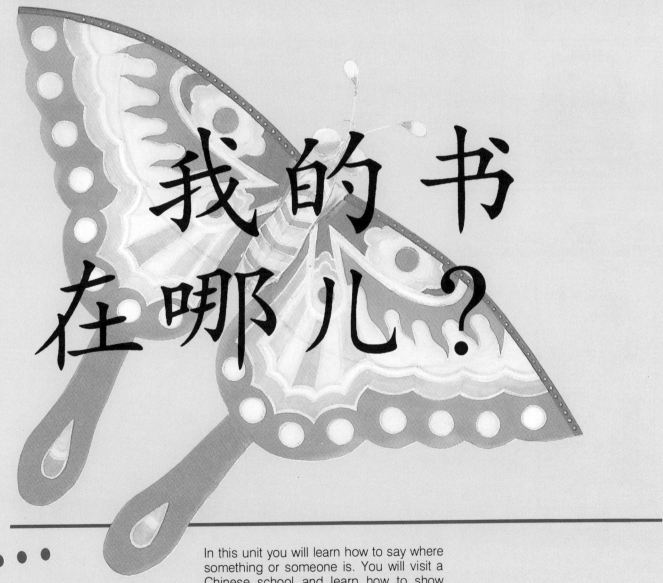

我的书
在哪儿?

In this unit you will learn how to say where something or someone is. You will visit a Chinese school and learn how to show someone around your own school. You will also learn how to exchange addresses with a new acquaintance.

3.1 Indicating where someone or something is

● 在哪儿？ (Zài nǎr?)

咪咪 在 桌子 上面。
mīmī zhuō mian

咪咪 在 桌子 下面。
mīmī zhuō mian

非非 在 汽车 里面。
fēifēi qì lǐmiàn

咪咪 在 汽车 外面。
mīmī qì wàimian

咪咪 在 非非 前面。
mīmī fēifēi qiánmian

非非 在 咪咪 后面。
fēifēi mīmī hòumian

非非 在 王 太太 旁边。
fēifēi pángbiān

他们在哪儿？
妈妈 咪咪 姐姐
mīmī

咪咪 在 王 太太 和
mīmī

非非 对面。
fēifēi duìmiàn

Notes:

You can also use 边 biān (as in 旁边 pángbiān) with 上，下，里，外，前，后.

上边 shàngbian on top   下边 xiàbian beneath
里边 lǐbian inside   外边 wàibian outside
前边 qiánbian in front   后边 hòubian behind

哥哥 爸爸 弟弟
请问，他们在哪儿？

他们在哪儿？ →
Catch the mouse! → page 79

● 我们的教室楼
(Wǒmen de jiàoshìlóu)

Look at the illustration. Can you work out from what's being said here the meaning of *lóushàng* (楼上), *lóuxià* (楼下), *gébì* (隔壁) and *zhōngjiān* (中间)?

A. 1. 这 是 教室楼。
　　　　　　jiàoshìlóu

2. 王 老师 和 李 老师 在 楼下。
　　　　　　　　　　　　　　lóu

3. 萍萍、兰兰 和 建华 在 楼上。
　　píngpíng　lánlán　jiànhuá　lóu

B. 1. 萍萍、兰兰 和 建华 的 教室 在
　　píngpíng　lánlán　jiànhuá　jiàoshì

楼上。
lóu

2. 萍萍 的 教室 在 左边。
　　píngpíng　jiàoshì　zuǒbian

3. 建华 的 教室 在 右边。
　　jiànhuá　　　　　yòu

4. 兰兰 的 教室 在 中间。
　　lánlán　jiàoshì　jiān

C. 1. 王 老师 的 办公室 和
　　　　　　bàn shì

李 老师 的 办公室 都 在 楼下。
　　　　　　bàn shì　　　lóu

2. 李 老师 的 办公室
　lǐ　　　　bàn shì

Catch the mouse!
抓小老鼠！
(Zhuā xiǎo lǎoshǔ!)

Form two or three circles of eight persons each. In each circle, one person sits in the centre and assumes the role of the *xiǎo lǎoshǔ*. Everyone else is a *xiǎo māo*. The *xiǎo lǎoshǔ* secretly writes on a piece of paper where it is (for example, *Zài lǎoshī de zhuōzi xiàmian*). All the *xiǎo māo* then take turns in guessing where the *xiǎo lǎoshǔ* is. The 'mouse' replies to each 'cat' by saying, for example,

　Bù, wǒ bú zài . . .

or

　Duì, wǒ zài . . .

Whoever guesses correctly then says:

　Zhuādào le! (Caught you!)

The successful *xiǎo māo* then becomes the next *xiǎo lǎoshǔ*.

在 王 老师 办公室 的 隔壁。
　　　　bàn　　shì　　　　gébì

Notes:

Wáng lǎoshī hé Lǐ lǎoshī de bàngōngshì dōu zài lóuxià — In a school, *bàngōngshì* 办公室 (office) can also refer to the 'staff room'.

Here's how you say where you are in a building:

Wǒmen de jiàoshì	zài	lóushàng. lóuxià zhōngjiān gébì
Bàngōngshì	zài	jiàoshì　　　de gébì.

你的办公室在哪儿？　→
你听懂了吗？　→

● 说汉语（一）🔘

1. 阿伦：李 老师 在 吗？
　　ālún　　lǐ

　　琳达：不 在，他 回 办公室 了。
　　líndá　　　　　　　　bàn　　shì

　　阿伦：他 的 办公室 在 哪儿？
　　　　　　　　　bàn　　shì

　　琳达：就 在 对面 那个 楼，二 层。
　　　　　　　　　miàn　　　　lóu　　　céng

2. 王 老师：你 找 谁？

　　阿伦：找 李 老师。
　　　　　　　lǐ

　　王 老师：李 老师……，他 在 那头儿，
　　　　　　　lǐ

你的办公室在哪儿？

Work with a partner. Each choose one of the rooms in the *jiàoshìlóu* as your own and write down its location on a piece of paper without showing your partner. Then try to guess correctly where each other's office is located. The only question that cannot be asked is:

Nǐ de bàngōngshì zài nǎr?

你听懂了吗？🔘

True or false?

1. a) The boy wanted to know where David was.
   b) He wanted to know where Xiaoming was.
   c) He wanted to know where Xiaoming's mother was.

2. a) The boy does not know who David is.
   b) He knows David quite well.

在 右边，好象 是 五 号 房间。
yòubian　xiàng　　　　　fángjiān

阿伦： 谢谢！
ālún

王老师： 不 客气。

Notes:

Jiù zài duìmiàn nèige lóu — Jiù (就) may be used for emphasis as it is here. More examples:

Zhèr jiù shì Lǐ lǎoshī de bàngōngshì.
Wǒ jiù zhù zhèr.

Find the Chinese →
怎么说? →

LEARN TO READ   page 100

LEARN TO WRITE   Lesson 11   page 111

Find the Chinese

It's in that building opposite, on the first floor.
Who are you looking for?
Is Mr Li there please?
I think it's Room 5.
I want to see Mr Li.
He's down that end, on the right.
He's gone back to his office.

怎么说?

When Linda tells Alan where Mr Li's office is, to make her reply more emphatic she says:

就在 ······ (*Jiù zài*) ...

instead of just:

在 ······ (*Zài* ...)

How would you tell someone that the place they are looking for is:
• Room 7 downstairs?
• that office on the left?
• next to Mr Smith's office?
• upstairs opposite the classroom?
• in the building ahead?
For example, you could say:

Jiù zài lóuxià 7 hào fángjiān.

3.2   What are they doing there?

● 你猜猜看！  (Nǐ cāicāi kàn!)

保罗： 你 正在 做 什么？
bǎoluó

安娜： 我 正在 复习 功课。
　　　　　　　fùxí　gōng

保罗： 你 猜 我 正在 做 什么？
　　　　cāi

安娜： 我 怎么 知道？

保罗： 猜猜 看。
　　　cāicāi

安娜： 你 …… 正在 看 书。
ānnà

保罗： 不 对！
bǎoluó

安娜： 你 正在 画 画儿。
　　　　　　　huà　huà

保罗： 没有，我 没有 画 画儿。
　　　　　　　　　　huà　huà

安娜： 你 正在 听 音乐。
　　　　　　　　yīnyuè

保罗： 没有，我 没有 听 音乐。
　　　　　　　　　　yīnyuè

安娜： 咳，我 猜不着！
　　　hāi　　cāi　zháo

保罗： 我 在 打 电话 呢！

安娜： 你 呀，正在 讨人嫌！
　　　ya　　　　tǎo xián

Notes:

1. *Hāi, wǒ cāibùzháo!* — *Hāi* (咳) is an exclamation expressing sadness or surprise or, as in this case, regret mixed with impatience.
   More examples:

   Hāi, xià yǔ le, jīntiān bù néng dǎ qiú le!
   Hāi, tā shì lǎoshī? Wǒ yǐwéi tā shì xuésheng ne!

   In which of the above two examples is the speaker expressing surprise and in which one regret?

2. *Wǒ zài dǎ diànhuà ne!* — This is the same as saying *Wǒ zhèngzài dǎ diànhuà*. Note that:
   a) *Zài* (在) may be used by itself to indicate that an action is happening, and
   b) *Ne* (呢) also indicates that the action is happening and may be used by itself in a sentence. For example:

      Ānnà shuìjiào ne! (Anna is sleeping!)

c) *Zhèng* (正) may also be used by itself.
Therefore, the following five sentences *all* indicate that the action is progressing or continuing (i.e. that someone is revising or reviewing his or her schoolwork):

Tā	zhèngzài	fùxí gōngkè.	
Tā	zhèng	fùxí gōngkè.	
Tā	zài	fùxí gōngkè.	
Tā		fùxí gōngkè.	ne.
Tā	zhèngzài	fùxí gōngkè.	ne.

Find the Chinese

I give up!
How should I know?
Have a guess.
Can you guess what I'm doing?
You're being annoying!
No, I'm not drawing.

Find the Chinese →

他们 在 那儿 做 什么?

(Tāmen zài nàr zuò shénme?)

1. 保罗 在 球场 上 打 球。
   bǎoluó   chǎng

2. 安娜 在 她 的 房间 里 看 书。
   ānnà   lǐ

3. 妈妈 在 车站 等 朋友。
            zhàn děng

4. 姐姐 在 家 里 做 健身操。
            lǐ   jiànshēncāo

5. 爸爸 在 汽车 里 等 人。
                lǐ děng

6. 李 老师 在 图书馆 里 看 书。
   lǐ   tú guǎn lǐ

Notes:

1. Notice that -miàn (-面) in lǐmiàn (里面), shàngmian (上面) is often omitted. For example:

    Tā zài fángjiān lǐ(miàn) zuò shénme?

2. The zài (在) in zài qiúchǎng shàng (在球场上) means 'on' (indicating position or location) and should not be confused with zài (在) in zhèngzài (正在) (although they look the same)!

Tā	**zài**	fángjiān lǐ(miàn)	zuò shénme?
Tā	**zài**	fángjiān lǐ(miàn)	zuò zuòyè fùxí gōngkè

When you want to say that the place referred to is not the one where the action is happening, you use this pattern:

Tā	**bú**	zài	fángjiān lǐ(miàn)	zuò zuòyè. fùxí gōngkè

3. *Bàba zài qìchē lǐ děng rén* — *Rén* is used here to mean 'somebody'.

想一想 →
我正在做什么？ →
Crazy sentences →

● 说汉语（二）

1. 安娜：   喂？
   ānnà   wèi

   小明：   喂！你 是 安娜 吧？
   　　　　 wèi　　　　　ānnà

   安娜：   是，你 是
   ānnà

   　　　　 小明 吧？

想一想

Is the zài (在) in each of these sentences the zài in zhèngzài (正在) or the zài in zài (在……) which indicates location?

- *Dàwèi zài xiě zì.*
- *Māma zài shuìjiào.*
- *Bàba zài fángjiān lǐ.*
- *Jiějie de péngyou zài nǎr?*

How can you tell?

我正在做什么？

1. In turn, one or more students mime an action in front of the class. The class says what the action is. For example:

    Dàwèi zhèngzài mǎi dōngxi.

2. This time, whoever is miming an action, also conveys *where* the action is taking place and the class says what the person is doing and where. For example:

    Ānnà zài chēzhàn děng péngyou.

Crazy sentences

Work in pairs. Together make up as many sentences as you can think of in the pattern of:

Láolā zài hǎibiānr yóuyǒng.

Now cut up the sentences you have written. For example:

Láolā / zài hǎibiānr / yóuyǒng

and put the pieces in three piles labelled 'Who', 'Where' and 'What', scrambling them as you do so. Then take it in turns to pick one piece from each pile and read the whole sentence out. Some of the results may surprise you!

小明：　是。

安娜：　你 好 吗？
ānnà

小明：　挺 好 的。你 哥哥 在家 吗？

安娜：　在，他 在 房间 里 玩 电子 游戏。
　　　　　　　　　　　　　 lǐ　　　　　 yóuxì

小明：　请 他 接 电话，好 吗？
　　　　　　　 jiē

安娜：　好，请 你 等 一下儿，
　　　　　　　　　 děng

　　　　　我 去 叫 他。

2. 阿伦：　喂？
　 ālún　 wèi

小明：　喂，阿伦，我 的 墨镜
　　　　 wèi　 ālún　　　 mòjìng

　　　　　在 你 那儿 吗？

阿伦：　你 的 墨镜？没有 啊。
　 ālún　　　　 mòjìng

安娜：　墨镜？
　　　　 mòjìng

　　　　　外面 桌子 上 有 一 副 墨镜。
　　　　 wài　 zhuō　　　　　 fù　 mòjìng

阿伦：　你 等 一 等。
　　　　　 děng　 děng

　　　　……

有 了! 在 我 们 这 儿 呢!

小明： 太 好 了! 谢 谢!

Notes:

1. *Zài nǐ nàr ma?* — If you want to express such concepts as 'at Alan's', 'at Mary's', 'at your place' or 'at my place', you use *zài* (在). However, since *zài* requires a place or location as its object, you say *Ālún nàr*, *Mǎlì nàr*, *nǐ nàr*, *wǒ zhèr*. These expressions mean literally 'the place where Alan is', 'the place where you are' and so on.
   Note that this also applies when verbs such as *qù* (去), and *lái* (来) are used. For example;

   Wǒ xiǎng qù Ālún nàr.   I'm going to Alan's (place).
   Tā míngtiān lái wǒ zhèr.   She's coming to my place tomorrow.

2. *Wàimian zhuōzi shàng yǒu yí fù mòjìng* — *Yǒu* (有) indicates existence in this sentence and has the sense of 'there is' or 'there are'.

Find the Chinese   →
我的墨镜在你那儿吗?   →

LEARN TO READ   page 101

LEARN TO WRITE   Lesson 12   page 112

Find the Chinese

Wait a minute.
Is your brother at home?
There's a pair of sunglasses on the table outside.
They're here! At our place!
I'll go and get him.
All right, just a minute.
He's in his room playing video games.
Could I speak to him, please? (on the phone)

我的墨镜在你那儿吗?

Work in pairs. Role-play ringing a friend to ask if something you have misplaced is at their place.
Record your dialogue and listen to it or act out your dialogue in front of the class.

3.3   Talking about your school

Chinese children attend primary school (小学 *xiǎoxué*) at the age of 6 or 7 for five or six years. Then they go to high school (中学 *zhōngxué*) which lasts for another six years after which they may continue their studies at a university (大学 *dàxué*) or institute (学院 *xuéyuàn*).

Li Fang.attends the No. 40 high school in Beijing. It is quite a large school with over 1000 students, some of whom are boarders. They have classes for six days of the week and have a day off on Sundays. A typical school day begins at 7.30 in the morning and ends at about 5.00 in the afternoon. There are four 45-minute periods in the morning and two or three in the afternoon.

There is a lunch break at 12.00 followed by a midday nap (in the hot summer months). Li Fang brings her own lunch of rice and steamed buns with some vegetables and meat or fish in a lunch box. She leaves it at the school kitchen or boiler-room where it is heated for lunchtime. Those who live nearby might go home for lunch.

Much attention is placed on the physical well-being of the students. Students and teachers take part in mid-morning group exercises and are encouraged to participate in after-school sport activities such as basketball and volleyball.

● 李方的学校 (Lǐ Fāng de xuéxiào)

我 叫 李方。这 是 我 的 学校。
lǐ

我们 学校 有 教室楼，有 小卖部，有 办公室，
　　　　　　　　　　　　　mài bù

图书馆，
tú guǎn

礼堂，
lǐtáng

还 有 操场
cāochǎng

和 球场。
chǎng

这 是 我们 的 教室楼。　　　这 是 学校 的 大门。
我 的 教室 在 这儿。　　　　　　　　　　　　mén

门口 附近 有 车站。
ménkǒu fùjìn　　zhàn

这 是 我们 的 礼堂。
lǐtáng

这 是 图书馆，我们 的 图书馆 有 很多 书。
tú guǎn　　　　　　 tú guǎn

教室楼 对面 有 小卖部。
mài bù

球场 在 教室楼 后面。
chǎng   hòu

操场 在 球场 旁边。
cāochǎng   chǎng pángbiān

我们 喜欢 在 教室楼 后面 打 乒乓球。
hòu   pīngpāng

厕所 在 那儿。
cèsuǒ

男 厕所 在 左边。
nán cèsuǒ   zuǒbian

女 厕所 在 右边。
cèsuǒ   yòubian

Notes:

You have already learnt to use the verb *yǒu* (有) to indicate 'possession' or 'to have'. For example:

> *Wǒ yǒu zìxíngchē.*
> *Wǒ yǒu yí gè Zhōngguó péngyou.*

Yǒu is also used to indicate the *existence* of something, as in these sentences which you have learnt.

> *Nǐ jiā yǒu jǐ gè rén?*
> *Wàimian zhuōzi shàng yǒu yí fù mòjìng(r).*

When used this way, *yǒu* acquires the meaning of 'There is ...', 'There are ...' (or 'There was/were ...' or 'There will be ...'). In such sentences *yǒu* is preceded by words indicating a location or time. For example:

Location/time		
Ménkǒu fùjìn	**yǒu**	chēzhàn.
Jiàoshì lǐ		rén.
Jiàoshìlóu duìmiàn		xiǎomàibù.
Zuótiān wǎnshang		rén zhǎo nǐ.
Míngtiān		yǔ.

Such sentences are made negative by using *méiyǒu* (没有). For example:

Fángjiān lǐmiàn Zhuōzi shàngmian	**méiyǒu**	rén. shū.

More about your school

校长办公室 xiàozhǎng bàngōngshì *principal's office*
小礼拜堂 xiǎo lǐbàitáng *chapel*
实验室 shíyànshì *laboratory*
体育馆 tǐyùguǎn *gymnasium*
食堂 shítáng *refectory*
音乐室 yīnyuèshì *music room*
电脑室 diànnǎoshì *computer room*
金工室 jīngōngshì *metalwork room*
视听室 shìtīngshì *A.V. room*
木工室 mùgōngshì *woodwork room*
美术室 měishùshì *art room*
绘图室 huìtúshì *technical drawing room*
停车场 tíngchēchǎng *carpark*

● 请问，办公室在哪儿？
(Qǐngwèn, bàngōngshì zài nǎr?)

1. 王勇： 请问，谁 是 陈 老师？
   yǒng   chén

   安娜： 陈 老师 是 我们 的 汉语
   ānnà   chén

   老师。你 找 他 有 事儿 吗?

   王勇： 有，我 找 他 有 事儿。
   yǒng

   他 的 办公室 在 哪儿？

   彼得： 在 图书馆 旁边。
   bǐ   tú   guǎn pángbiān

2. 王勇： 那，……图书馆 在 哪儿 呢？
   yǒng   tú   guǎn

   安娜： 你 是 新生 吧？
   ānnà   xīn

   王勇： 是，我 是 新生……。
                  xīn

   彼得： 欢迎，欢迎！我 来 介绍 一下儿，
   bǐ   yíng   yíng   jièshào

我 叫 彼得。这 是 安娜。
　　　 bǐ　　　　　　　ānnà

王勇： 你们 好！我 叫 王 勇。
yǒng

彼得： 你 好！
bǐ

安娜： 你 好！我们 带 你 去 吧！
ānnà

3. 安娜： 办公室 在 这个 楼 里。
　　　　　　　　　　　　　 lǐ

陈 老师 的 办公室 在 一 层。
chén

彼得： 你 看，陈 老师 在 那儿 呢！

安娜： 陈 老师！

4. 陈 老师： 彼得，安娜，有 事儿 吗？
chén

彼得： 陈 老师，这 是 王 勇。他 是 新生。
bǐ　　　　　　　　　　　　　　　　　　 xīn

安娜： 他 找 您 有 事儿。
　　　　　　　 nín

陈 老师： 哦，(to Wang Yong) 请 进！

5. 王 勇： (to Anna and Peter) 谢谢 你们。
yǒng

彼得： 不用 谢。

安娜，彼得：再见!

　　ānnà

王勇：再见!

　　yǒng

Find the Chinese　→
你听懂了吗?　→

● 说汉语（三）

Draw a map of your school as accurately as you can, showing the entrance, buildings, pathways, playing fields, office, carpark and so on. Plan a tour of the school (the route and the names of the various items of interest), then take one or a group of 'visitors' around the school grounds. Remember, the visitor(s) will be asking you questions during the tour!

● 你上几年级?

(Nǐ shàng jǐ niánjí?)

High school, or *zhōngxué* (中学), is usually divided into junior high school and senior high school in China. Junior high is called *chūzhōng* (初中) and runs for three years. Senior high is called *gāozhōng* (高中) and also runs for three years.

李方：你是新生吧?
 lǐ　　　　　 xīn

张云：是。
zhāng yún

李方：欢迎，欢迎! 我叫李方。
 lǐ　　　yíng　　yíng　　　　 lǐ

张云：我叫张云。你也是新生
zhāng yún　　　 zhāng yún　　　　　 xīn

　　　吗?

李方：不是。
 lǐ

张云：你上几年级?
　　　　　　　　　 jǐ

Find the Chinese

Mr Chen's office is on the ground floor.
Did you want to see me?
We'll take you there.
Look, there's Mr Chen.
Do you want to see him about something?
So, . . . where's the library?
The staff rooms are in this building.
He wants to see you about something.

你听懂了吗?

True or false?

1. a) i) There is a total of six basketball courts at the boy's school.
   ii) There are only four courts.
   b) i) Two of the courts are in front of the classroom building.
   ii) Two of the courts are behind the classroom building.
   iii) Two of the courts are behind the tuckshop.
   c) i) Teacher Li was in his office.
   ii) He was playing basketball.

2. a) i) The girl found a pair of shorts in the boy's schoolbag.
   ii) The girl did not find any shorts in the boy's schoolbag.
   b) i) There was a pair of shorts on the chair in the boy's room.
   ii) There was a pair of shorts on the desk in the boy's room.
   c) i) It was a rather cold day.
   ii) It was a hot day.

李 方： 我 上 初二。
li   chū

张 云： 你们 的 教室 在 哪儿?

李 方： 在 楼上，我 在 三 班。
                                 bān

         你 呢? 你 在 哪个 班?
                               bān

张 云： 我 在 初一 十二 班。
zhāng yún   chū   bān

         我们 在 楼下。

Notes:

Wǒ shàng chū'èr — *Chū'èr* (初二) is an abbreviation of *chūzhōng èr niánjí* (初中二年级) which means 'Grade 2 of junior high school'.

该你了! →
你听懂了吗? →

● 说汉语 (四)

李 方： 诶，你 看，谁 的 书包?
lǐ   éi   bāo

张 云： 不 知道。
zhāng yún

李 方： 打开 看看。
lǐ   kāi

张 云： 是 陈 新 的。
zhāng yún   chén xīn

李 方： 陈 新? 我 不 认识。
lǐ   chén xīn   rènshi

该你了

Role-play a meeting between a student and a new student at the school entrance. The new student is looking for the school office.

     Perform your role play in front of the class or record your role play and listen to it.

你听懂了吗?

1. Paul knew that Caroline was a new student when:
   a) She told him that she was new to the school.
   b) She did not know where the classroom building was.
   c) She did not know where the library was.

2. True or false?
   a) The Year 8 and Year 9 students share the same building.
   b) The Year 8 building and Year 9 building are next door to each other.
   c) The library is close by.

3. True or false?
   a) They are both in Year 9.
   b) Caroline and Paul are both in Year 8.
   c) Caroline is in Year 8 and Paul is in Year 9.

4. True or false?
   a) Caroline and Paul are classmates.
   b) They are not classmates.

张 云： 我 也 不 认识。
zhāng yún　　　　　　　rènshi

看 他 的 字，好 象 是 男 的。
　　　　　　　　　　xiàng　　nán

李 方： 他 在 哪 个 班？
lǐ　　　　　　　　　bān

张 云： 我 看 看，…… 初 二 三 班。
zhāng yún　　　　　　chū　　bān

李 方： 哦，我 记 起 来 了，是 男 的，
lǐ　　　　　jì　　　　　　　　nán

个 子 挺 高 的，戴 眼 镜 儿。
　　　　　　　　dài　　yǎnjìngr

李 方： 这 个 书 包 ……。
lǐ　　　　　　　bāo

张 云： 交 给 老 师 吧。
zhāng yún　　jiāo

李 方： 好。

Find the Chinese

He wears glasses.
I don't know Chen Xin.
What class is he in?
Now I remember him.
It looks like a boy's handwriting.
He's quite tall.
(Open it and) have a look inside.
Let's hand it in to a teacher.
He's in Form 2C.

Notes:

Kàn tā de zì, hǎoxiàng shì nán de — Zì (字) may be used to refer to one's handwriting. For example:

Nǐ xiě ba, nǐ de zì zhēn hǎokàn.

Find the Chinese →
该你了 →

LEARN TO READ　page 103

LEARN TO WRITE　**Lesson 13**　page 113

该你了

Role-play the situation in the 说汉语四 dialogue with a partner. Change the dialogue so that the description is of someone in your grade, but give this person a fictitious name (for example, *Tuōní Shǐmìsī* — Tony or Toni Smith). Perform your role play in front of the class and see if the rest of the class can identify the 'mystery' person.

3.4 Indicating a change

下雨了！
(Xià yǔ le!)

他 高兴 了！
xìng

下 雨 了！
yǔ

没 有 了！

你 懂 了 吗?

老师 不 来 了！

我 瘦 了！
shòu

我 不 游泳 了！

该你了！ (Gāi nǐ le!)

What situations would give rise to these statements?

1. 我的衣服小了！
2. 天气冷了。
3. 你胖了！
4. 我现在不喜欢他了。
5. 他不是学生了。
6. 不刮风了。
   guā fēng
7. 我不去了。
8. 你们听吧。我不听了。
9. 你爸爸回家了。
10. 车站不在这儿了。
    zhàn

Notes:

Xià yǔ le! — *Le* (了) may be used to indicate that there has been a *change* in circumstances. The changes indicated may vary. For example *le* may indicate:

● the emergence of new circumstances *Xià yǔ le! / Wǒ è le!*
● that something is about to happen *Kuài xià yǔ le!*
● that an action has come to a halt *Tā bù shuōhuà le.*
● a change in characteristics or state *Xiànzài tā jiào Dàwèi le.*
● a change in one's intentions *Wǒ bù xiǎng qù le.*
● a change in number *Tā jīnnián 12 suì le.*

Note that used in this way, *le* generally appears at the end of a sentence.

该你了！ →

● 我记不起来了 [cassette]

(Wǒ jì bù qilai le)

1. 王华： 这个 词 是 什么 意思？
   huá   cí   yìsi

   林英： 我 记 不 起 来 了。
   yīng   jì

   去 问问 李 老师 吧。
   lǐ

   王 华： 好。

2. 王 华： 李 老师，这 句 话 我 不
   lǐ   jù

   太 懂。

   李 老师： 我 看看。

   王 华： 这个 词 是 什么 意思？
   cí   yìsi

   李 老师： 'Extremely' 是 "非常" 的 意思。
   yìsi

   王 华： 哦，我 明白 了!
   这 句 话 的 意思 是
   jù   yìsi

   "他 非常 高兴。"

   老师： 对。

3. 林 英： 怎么样？
   yīng

   王 华： 老师 说 'extremely' 是 "非常" 的 意思。
   yìsi

Find the Chinese

How did it go?
I don't quite understand this sentence.
I can't remember.
Now I understand.
Why don't you go and ask the teacher?
What does this word mean?
'Extremely' means 'fēicháng'.
Let me have a look.

Vocabulary bee

Two teams take turns asking each other the meaning of a Chinese word. (*Zhèige cí shì shénme yìsi?*) A team wins a point by answering correctly and loses a point if a team member cannot answer or uses English. Team members who cannot remember the meaning of the word but who correctly use the phrase

我记不起来了

can win their team half a point.
   The vocabulary bee can be extended to include asking the meaning of sentences (*Zhèi jù huà shì shénme yìsi?*) or of individual characters (*Zhèige zì shì shénme yìsi?*)

你听懂了吗？ [cassette]

True or false?

1. a) The people were trying to arrange to meet each other.
   b) They were trying to decide where to go.
   c) They were deciding on when to go out together.

2. a) They had good weather that day, but it started raining.
   b) It had been raining for the last couple of days.
   c) It was a fine day.

3. a) Dianne suggested that they go today.
   b) She suggested that they go tomorrow.
   c) She said she did not care.

Find the Chinese → page 95
Vocabulary bee → page 95
你听懂了吗? → page 95

● 说 汉语（五）🔘

安娜: 诶，我 的 书 在 哪儿 了?
ānnà   éi

刚才 还 在 这儿。

保罗: 你 想 一 想。
bǎoluó

安娜: 我 记 不 起来 了!
ānnà   jì

保罗: 我 帮 你 找找。
bǎoluó

马克: 你们 找 什么?
mǎkè

安娜: 我 的 书。

马克: 在 我 这儿 呢!

你 忘 了? 昨天 你 借给
       wàng

我 了。

安娜: 哦，对 了。我 记 起来 了!
          jì

Find the Chinese →
该你了! →

LEARN TO READ page 105
LEARN TO WRITE Lesson 14 page 114

4. a) It was decided that Peter would call Chen Xin.
   b) It was decided that Dianne would call Chen Xin.

5. a) Chen Xin preferred to go that afternoon.
   b) She had no objections to going the next day.

Find the Chinese

That's right. Now I remember.
Try to remember.
I've got it.
Don't you remember?
Hey, where's my book?
You lent it to me yesterday.
I'll help you look for it.
It was here just now.
I can't remember.

该你了! (Gāi nǐ le!)

Work in pairs. Make up a role play where an absent-minded person (A) cannot find his or her belongings and person B has to keep reminding A what he or she did with whatever it is A is looking for. You could use phrases such as:

   Éi, wǒ de . . . zài nǎr le?
   Gāngcái hái zài zhèr!
   Nǐ wàng le? Zuótiān nǐ . . .

Be inventive!
   Perform your role play in front of the class or record your role play and listen to it.

3.5 Giving someone your address

● 我们也住花园路 [cassette icon]

(Wǒmen yě zhù Huāyuán Lù)

| 大卫： | 我们 可以 帮 您 的 忙 吗？ |
| | wèi   nín   máng |

林 太太：哦，不用 了，谢谢！

我 家 就 在 前面。

| 劳拉： | 是 花园 路 吗？ |
| | láolā   huāyuán   lù |

林 太太：是。

| 大卫： | 我们 也 住 花园 路。 |
| | wèi   huāyuán   lù |

| 劳拉： | 来，我们 帮 您 拿 吧。 |
| | láolā   nín |

林 太太：好，好，谢谢！

劳拉： 没 什么。

林 太太：你们 会 说 中国话？

大卫： 会 一点儿，

我们 学校 有 汉语课。

| 林 太太：哦，真 有 意思！ |
| | yìsi |

你 叫 什么 名字？

大卫： 我 叫 大卫。这 是……。

劳拉： 我 叫 劳拉。您 贵 姓？
láolā   láolā   nín   guì   xìng

林 太太： 我 姓 林。……
         xìng

到 了，这 是 我 的 家。
dào

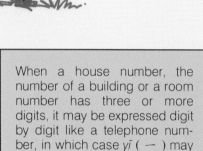

劳拉： 哦，您 住 十 四 号。
láolā   nín

我们 住 二 十 七 号。
林 太太： 进来 坐 一 坐 吧！
劳拉： 不用 了，我们 得 回家 做 功课。
         gōng

林 太太： 那 你们 有 空儿 来 玩儿 啊！
劳拉： 好。
大卫，劳拉： 再见！
林 太太： 再见！

Find the Chinese →

● 说汉语（六）

马克： 你 知道 安 的 电话 号码 吗？
mǎkè   ān   mǎ

琳达： 干吗？
líndá   gànmá

When a house number, the number of a building or a room number has three or more digits, it may be expressed digit by digit like a telephone number, in which case yī (一) may be pronounced as yāo （幺）
For example:

> Wǒmen zhù Běijīng Lù 214 (èr-yāo-sì) hào.

However, a number below one hundred is *always* expressed as a whole number. For example:

> Shí'èr hào rather than yī-èr hào.

Tā zhù 18 (shíbā) hào, wǒmen jiā zhù 16 (shíliù) hào.

Wǒ de dìzhǐ shi Dàtóng Lù 71 (qīshíyī) hào.

Find the Chinese

Here, we'll help you carry these.
Here we are, this is my place.
It's nothing. (*polite response to thanks*)
What is your name? (*polite*)
We live in Garden Road too.
Please come in for a while!
Come and visit when you have some free time then!
Can we help you?
Thanks all the same but we have to go home to do our schoolwork.
In Garden Road?
Our school teaches Chinese.
My place is just up ahead.

马克: 我 有 事儿 找 她。
mǎkè

琳达: 她 家 好象 没有 电话。
líndá   xiàng

马克: 你 知道 她 住 哪儿 吗?
mǎkè

琳达: 她 住 东南 区。
líndá   nán qū

马克: 你 有 她 的
    地址 吗?
        dìzhǐ

琳达: 我 看看, ……
    她 的 地址 是 花园 路 12 号。
        dìzhǐ   shì huāyuán lù

马克: 谢谢。
琳达: 不 谢。

Notes:

1. *Gànmá?* — This is a colloquial way of saying *Gàn shénme?*
2. *Tā de dìzhǐ shì Huāyuán Lù 12 hào* — Note that the name of the street comes first, followed by the house number.

Find the Chinese →
怎么说? →

LEARN TO READ   page 107

LEARN TO WRITE   Lesson 15   page 115

Find the Chinese

I don't think they have the telephone on at her place.
Why do you want it?
She lives in the Southeast District.
I have to see her about something.
Do you have her address?

怎么说?

The 东 in 东南区 is a character you have already met in 东西, meaning 'thing', and you know that the other part of this compound (西) means 'west'. In *Hanyu for Beginning Students* you met the character 北 (north) in 北京. So now that you have met the character for 'south' (南) you know all the four directions of the compass!

What do you notice about the way 'southeast' is expressed in Chinese compared to the way it is expressed in English? How do you think you would express the following (in Chinese)?

- northeast
- southwest
- northwest

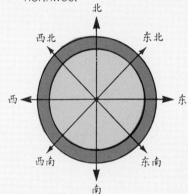

你住哪儿? 🔲

Here are some more words you might need when talking about where you live:

街 jiē *street*
巷 xiàng *lane*
邮政编码 yóuzhèng biānmǎ *post code*

学会认字 (Xuéhuì rèn zì)

3.1

Before reading the text, listen to the recording and answer the questions.

True or false?
1. It is likely that the boy and the girl are foreign students in China.
2. They wanted to see Teacher Lin.
3. They were not familiar with the school grounds.
4. The man who first gave them directions was wrong.
5. Teacher Lin's office is located on the ground floor.

● 汉字表

				As in
办	bàn	to do, handle, manage	办公楼
楼	lóu	storeyed building	
前	qián	front	前面
面	miàn	face; side; aspect	
室	shì	room	办公室
层	céng	storey; floor; layer, (measure word)	二层
教	jiào	to instruct, teach	教室
房	fáng	room; house	房间
间	jiān	room	
哦	ò	(exclamatory word)	哦，我知道了！

Text 📼

a) G: 请问，办公楼在哪儿？

M: 前面那个楼就是办公楼。

B: 你知道林老师的办公室在哪儿吗？

M: 在一层。

G: 谢谢。

M: 不谢。

b) (On the first floor)

G: 这层怎么都是教室呢？

B: 是啊，怎么回事儿？

　……

W: 你们找谁啊？

G: 林老师。

W: 林老师在楼下，一〇五号房间。

B: 这儿不是一层吗？

W: 不是，这是二层。

B: 二层？这怎么是二层呢？！

W: 哦，我知道了。

　你们的一层是我们的二层！

G: 哦，我明白了！

　谢谢。

　(to B) 走吧！

B: 我还不明白。

3.2

Before reading the text, listen to the recording and answer the questions.

Dialogue 1
True or false?
1. The dialogue took place at home.
2. Mum did not approve of her daughter's outfit.
3. The girl had put on something that was quite popular and fashionable.
4. The boy did not hear his mother's comment on his sister's clothes.

Dialogue 2
True or false?
1. The family lived in a single-storey house.
2. Mum was listening to music.
3. She was doing an aerobics routine.
4. The boy and girl had never seen their mother doing aerobics before.

动动脑筋
(Dòngdong nǎojīn)

1. What sort of person would be one described as

怕事儿？

2. Is it a good thing if there's lots of

好人好事

in your school?

3. Someone described as

高高在上

would be
a) very tall?
b) living in a high-rise apartment?
c) aloof and far removed from reality?

● 汉字表

			As in
等	děng	to wait	正在等；等一会儿
肥	féi	fat; (of clothing) loose	裤子太肥了
难	nán	unpleasant; difficult	难看；难学
髦	máo	fashionable	时髦
音	yīn	sound	音乐
乐	yuè	music	
猜	cāi	to guess	你猜她正在做什么？
健	jiàn	to strengthen; healthy	健身
操	cāo	drill; exercise	健身操

Text 🔊

1. 妈妈：　你正在做什么？
   哥哥：　我正在等小明呢。
   　　　　他一会儿就来我们家。
   妈妈：　妹妹呢？
   哥哥：　她在房间里穿衣服呢。

(Sister comes out of her room)

   妹妹：　你们说，好看不好看？
   妈妈：　你穿什么衣服啊？
   　　　　太肥了！半长不短的，
   　　　　真难看！
   哥哥：　谁说难看？
   　　　　我们现在都喜欢这个样子。
   妈妈：　你们孩子啊，就喜欢赶时髦！

2. 妹妹：　妈妈在哪儿？
   哥哥：　在楼下。

想一想

1. In the dialogue Mum describes the clothing as

   半长不短

   a) What do you think it means?
   b) How would you express the idea in English?

2. You have met the character 赶 in the phrase 赶作业, and the characters 时髦 in the phrase 不够时髦. What do you think this expression means?

   赶时髦

妹妹： 她在楼下做什么？

哥哥： 我不知道。

(Music is heard)

她正在听音乐吧。

(Sister goes downstairs, rushes up)

妹妹： 哥，你猜妈妈正在做什么？

哥哥： 我怎么知道？

妹妹： 你来看！

(They see Mum lying on the floor)

哥哥： 妈，你在做什么呢？

妈妈： 你说我正在做什么？

我正在做健身操。

哥哥： 健身操？你做健身操？

妈妈： 怎么啦？

我也在赶时髦！

动动脑筋

(Dòngdong nǎojīn)

1. Would you like to tackle a task that is said to be

难上难？

Why or why not?

2. Where would you expect to find this?

健身房

3.3

Before reading the text, listen to the recording and answer the questions.

True or false?
1. The boy had never been to the girl's school before.
2. He was quite impressed with the school grounds.
3. The offices are located in a grey building.
4. The girl does not like the library.
5. The tennis courts were behind the library.

● 汉字表

			As in
拍	pāi	*bat; racket*	球拍
些	xiē	*some; (measure word)*	那些大楼
灰	huī	*grey*	灰色
色	sè	*colour*	

右	yòu	right	右边
边	biān	side	
图	tú	picture; chart; map	图书馆
馆	guǎn	place for cultural activities	
后	hòu	behind; back; rear	后面
场	chǎng	place where people gather	球场
厕	cè	lavatory; toilet	厕所，女厕所
所	suǒ	place	
左	zuǒ	left	左边
男	nán	male person	男厕所

Text

1. G: 球拍拿了吗？

   B: 拿了。

   G: 走，现在就去我们学校。

2. G: 这就是我们学校。

   B: 真漂亮啊！……
      你们学校真大！

   G: 那个红色的大楼是办公楼，
      那些灰色的楼房都是教室楼。
      我们的教室楼在最右边。

   B: 哦。

3. B: 那个楼是什么？

   G: 是我们的图书馆。

   B: 你们的图书馆真大！

   G: 是挺大的，我们的图书馆书很多，
      我最喜欢在图书馆看书了！……

怎么样？你要看看我们的学校
还是要去打球？

B: 去打球吧。

G: 好，咱们现在去球场吧，
就在教室楼后面。

B: 等一等，我想上厕所。你们的厕
所在哪儿？

G: 厕所在对面，男厕所在左边。

动动脑筋
(Dòngdong nǎojīn)

1. What would you be doing in these places?

   a) 体育馆
   b) 饭馆
   c) 天文馆

2 How much would this be?

   六十左右

3.4

Before reading the text, listen to the recording and answer the questions.

Dialogue 1
True or false?
1. It has been a long time since Xiao Hong had seen Wang Li.
2. Wang Li and Xiao Hong went to school together.
3. Xiao Hong remembers Wang Li as being a rather tall and skinny boy.
4. Xiao Hong's brother was not at home.
5. Wang Li went to look for Xiao Hong's brother.

Dialogue 2
True or false?
1. The girl could not find her schoolbag.
3. The boy had taken the bag.
2. The boy told her to think again.
4. The bag was found lying beside the car.

● 汉字表

			As in
力	lì	strength	王力
瘦	shòu	thin; lean	他太瘦了！
戴	dài	to wear (hat, glasses, etc)	戴眼镜
镜	jìng	lens; mirror	眼镜
记	jǐ	remember	记起来
站	zhàn	station; stop; to stand	车站
包	bāo	bag; sack	书包
里	lǐ	in; inside	里面
忘	wàng	to forget	我忘了；健忘

Text 💿

1. 王力： 你是小红吧？

   林红： 是，你是……。

   王力： 我是你哥哥小学的同学王力。

   林红： 王力？

   王力： 我上小学的时候*没戴眼镜儿，
   现在是"四眼儿"了！

   林红： 哦，我记起来了。
   你现在个子高了，也瘦了！
   好久不见了，怎么样？好吗？

   王力： 挺好的，你呢？

   林红： 也挺好的。

   王力： 你哥哥在家吗？

   林红： 不在，他去车站等朋友了，
   一会儿就回来。你进来坐吧！

   王力： 不，我去找他，一会儿回来。

   林红： 好。…… 哦，你不用去了，
   你看，他们来了！

2. G: 我的书包怎么不见了？
   刚才还在这儿呢！

   B: 在这儿？你再想一想。

   G: 是，刚才就在这儿！

   M: 这个书包是谁的？

   G: 书包？在哪儿？

   *……的时候 means 'when…'.

动动脑筋

(Dòngdong nǎojīn)

1. Tell the class an experience of yours you would describe as

   难忘.

2. 健忘 means 'forgetful'. Where have you met the character 健 before?

M: 在汽车里面。

G: 哦，是我的……，我忘了。

B: 你怎么那么健忘啊！

3.5

Before reading the text, listen to the recording and answer the questions.

Dialogue 1
True or false?
1. The girl had told the boy her address before.
2. She lived in a large, white house.
3. The boy would have some difficulty finding her home.

Dialogue 2
1. The boy and the girl had not seen each other for a long time.
2. They had just met for the first time.
3. They exchanged addresses and telephone numbers.

● 汉字表

			As in
地	dì	place; locality	地址
址	zhǐ	location; site	
旁	páng	side	旁边
认	rèn	to recognise; know	认识
识	shí	to know	
兴	xìng	desire to do something	高兴
迎	yíng	to greet; welcome	欢迎

Text 🔄

1. 小红： 你有空儿来我家玩儿吧。

  王力： 好啊！

    哦，我忘了你们家的地址了！

    你的地址是……。

  小红： 东四三条十号。

王力： 三条……十号。

小红： 对，我家在白色的大楼旁边，
　　　　很好找。

王力： 好，我有空儿去找你！

小红： 再见！

王力： 再见！

2. B: 认识你，我很高兴！

G: 认识你，我也很高兴！

B: 这是我的地址和电话。
　　欢迎你有空儿来玩儿！

G: 好，谢谢。

动动脑筋

(Dòngdong nǎojīn)

1. 好找 means 'easy (or convenient) to find'. What do you think these phrases mean?

    a) 好做
    b) 好认
    c) 好办
    d) 好走

2. Someone is attending this lesson as a

    旁听生.

    What would that person be?

SUMMARY

(LTR stands for Learn to Read; LTW stands for Learn to Write)

3.1 Indicating where someone or something is

Now you can:

say where someone or something is:
Mīmī zài zhuōzi xiàmian. 咪咪在桌子下面。
Fēifēi zài Wáng tàitai pángbiānr.
　　非非在王太太旁边儿。
Tā zài nèi tóur,...zài yòubian.
　　他在那头儿，……在右边。
Tā de bàngōngshì zài duìmiàn nèige bàngōnglóu. 他的
办公室在对面那个办公楼。

describe where something is in a building:
Wáng lǎoshī de bàngōngshì zài lóuxià.
　　王老师的办公室在楼下。
Lǐ lǎoshī de bàngōngshì zài Wáng lǎoshī bàngōngshì de
　　gébì. 李老师的办公室在王老师办公室的隔壁。
Lánlán de jiàoshì zài zhōngjiān. 兰兰的教室在中间。

Useful phrases
Lǐ lǎoshī zài mà? 李老师在吗? *Is Teacher Li here?*
Nǐ zhǎo shéi? 你找谁? *Who are you looking for?*
Who do you want?
Hǎoxiàng shì wǔ hào fángjiān. 好象是五号房间。
I think it's Room 5.
(LTR) Zěnme huí shìr? 怎么回事儿? *Why do you ask?*
Why, what's the matter?

3.2 What are they doing there?

Now you can:

say where someone is and what they are doing there:
Tā zài jiā lǐ zuò jiànshēncāo. 她在家里做健身操。

Bǎoluó zài qiúchǎng shàng dǎ qiú.
保罗在球场上打球。

enquire if someone is home:
Nǐ gēge zàijiā ma? 你哥哥在家吗?

enquire if some article is at someone's place:
Wǒ de mòjìng zài nǐ nàr ma? 我的墨镜在你那儿吗?

possible reply:
Zài wǒmen zhèr ne! 在我们这儿呢!

Useful phrases
Yǒu le! 有了! *I've found it/them! They're here!*
Wǒ zěnme zhīdao? 我怎么知道? *How should I know?*
Cāicāi kàn. 猜猜看。 *Have a guess.*
Wǒ cāibùzháo. 我猜不着。 *I give up. (I can't guess.)*
Tài hǎo le! 太好了! *Wonderful! That's marvellous!*
(LTR) gǎn shímáo 赶时髦 *keep up with the fashions*
(LTR) bàn cháng bù duǎn 半长不短 *neither long nor short*
(LTR) Nǐ lái kàn! 你来看! *Come and look!*
(LTW) zài Xiǎo Míng nàr 在小明那儿 *at Xiao Ming's place*

3.3 Talking about your school

Now you can:

describe what there is at your school:
Wǒmen xuéxiào yǒu jiàoshìlóu, yǒu xiǎomàibù, yǒu bàngōngshì. 我们学校有教室楼，有小卖部，有办公室。
Xuéxiào ménkǒu fùjìn yǒu chēzhàn.
　　学校门口附近有车站。

offer to take someone somewhere:
Wǒmen dài nǐ qù ba! 我们带你去吧!

say you need to see someone about something:
Wǒ zhǎo tā yǒu shìr.   我找他有事儿。

ask what grade or class someone is in at school:
Nǐ shàng jǐ niánjí?   你上几年级?
Nǐ zài něige bān?   你在哪个班?

possible replies:
Wǒ shàng chū'èr.   我上初二。
Wǒ zài chūyī shi'èr bān.   我在初一十二班。

Useful phrases
Yǒu shìr ma?   有事儿吗?   *Did you want something?*
  Did you want to see me about something?
Wǒ jì qilai le.   我记起来了。   *Now I remember.*
(LTR) Zuì yòubian nèige lóu   最右边那个楼   *that build-ing on the far right*

Extra vocabulary
more places in your school   page 89

3.4   Indicating a change

Now you can:

describe a change:
Xià yǔ le!   下雨了!
Tā gāoxìng le!   他高兴了!
Wǒ bù yóuyǒng le!   我不游泳了!
Wǒ de shū zài nǎr le?   我的书在哪儿了?

ask the meaning of a word:
Zhèige cí shì shénme yìsi?   这个词是什么意思?

explain the meaning of a word or sentence:
"*Extremely*" shì "fēicháng" de yìsi.
    "*Extremely*" 是 "非常" 的意思。
Zhèi jù huà de yìsi shì "Tā fēicháng gāoxìng".
    这句话的意思是 "他非常高兴"。

puzzle over something's whereabouts:
(LTR) Wǒ de shūbāo zěnme bú jiàn le?   我的书包怎么
不见了?

Useful phrases
Wǒ jì bù qilai le.   我记不起来了。   *I can't remember. I've forgotten.*
Wǒ míngbai le.   我明白了。   *Now I understand.*
Zài wǒ zhèr.   在我这儿。   *I've got it (with/on me).*
(LTR) Nǐ búyòng qù le.   你不用去了。   *You needn't go. There's no need for you to go.*
(LTR) Nǐ xiǎng yì xiǎng.   你想一想。   *Think carefully. Think about it.*

3.5   Giving someone your address

Now you can:

offer to help someone:
Wǒmen kěyǐ bāng nín de máng ma?
    我们可以帮您的忙吗?
Wǒmen bāng nín ná ba.   我们帮您拿吧。

refuse or accept an offer of help:
Búyòng le, xièxie.   不用了,谢谢。
Hǎo, xièxie.   好,谢谢。

invite someone to come inside or to visit you some-time:
Jìnlai zuò yí zuò ba.   进来坐一坐吧!
Nǐ yǒu kòngr lái wánr a!   你有空儿来玩儿啊!

tell someone your address:
Wǒmen zhù èrshíqī hào.   我们住二十七号。
Tā de dìzhǐ shì Huāyuán Lù 12 hào.
    她的地址是花园路12号。

Useful phrases
Wǒ jiā jiù zài qiánmian.   我家就在前面。   *My house is just there. My house is just up ahead.*
Dào le.   到了。   *We're here. Here we are. (on arrival somewhere)*
Méi shénme.   没什么。   *(polite response to someone's thanks or apology)*
Búyòng le, ...   不用了,……   *Thanks all the same, . . . (polite refusal to an offer)*

Extra vocabulary
more words for addresses   page 99

学会写字 第十一课

(Xuéhuì xiě zì
Dì-shíyī kè)　　　　(3.1)

● 汉字表

请	qǐng *to request, ask; please; invite*	问	wèn *to ask*	办	bàn *to do, handle, manage*
公	gōng *public*	楼	lóu *storeyed building*	找	zhǎo *to look for*
房	fáng *room; house*	间	jiān *room*		

对话

A: 请问，这是办公楼吗？

B: 是，你找谁？

A: 王老师。

B: 王老师在一二五号房间。

学会写字 第十二课

(Xuéhuì xiě zì
Dì-shí'èr kè)   (3.2)

● 汉字表

见	jiàn *see*	书	shū *book*	教	jiào *teach, instruct*
室	shì *room*	外	wài *outside*	面	miàn *face; side; aspect*
跟	gēn *(preposition) with; and*				

对话 📼

A: 谁看见我的汉语书?

B: 在小明那儿。

A: 小明在哪儿?

B: 在教室外面。

他正在跟王老师说话。

学会写字 第十三课

(Xuéhuì xiě zì
Dì-shísān kè)   (3.3)

● 汉字表

Basic stroke

As in

漂	piào (as in piàoliang)	亮	liàng bright; light	前	qián front
色	sè colour	后	hòu behind; back; rear	场	chǎng place where people gather
课	kè class; lesson; subject				
常	cháng often				

短文 🔘🔘

　　这是我们的学校。我们的学校很大，很漂亮。前面那个白色的大楼是办公楼。那个大楼是我们的教室楼。教室楼后面是球场。

　　下了课，我们常常去球场打球。

学会写字 第十四课

(Xuéhuì xiě zì
Dì-shísì kè)

(3.4)

● 汉字表

对	duì right, correct; towards, to	久	jiǔ for a long time	怎	zěn how
样	yàng appearance, shape	挺	tǐng rather, quite; very	视	shì to look at
进	jìn to enter				

王星：对,我是王星,
　　　是你哥哥的小学同学。
蓝蓝：好久不见。怎么样,好
　　　吗?
王星：挺好的,你呢?
蓝蓝：也挺好的。
王星：你哥哥在家吗?
蓝蓝：在,他在房间里看电视
　　　呢。请进。

对话 📼

王星：你是小蓝吗?
蓝蓝：是。
王星：你长 (zhǎng) 高了!
蓝蓝：你是王星吧?

学会写字 第十五课

(Xuéhuì xiě zì
Dì-shíwǔ kè)   (3.5)

● 汉字表

认	rèn *to know recognise;*	识	shí *to know*	兴	xìng *desire to do something*
地	dì *place, locality*	址	zhǐ *location, site*		

对话

A: 认识你，我很高兴。

B: 认识你，我也很高兴。

A: 这是我的电话和地址。

B: 谢谢！

UNIT 4 | What subjects do you like doing?

第四单元

Dì-sì dānyuán

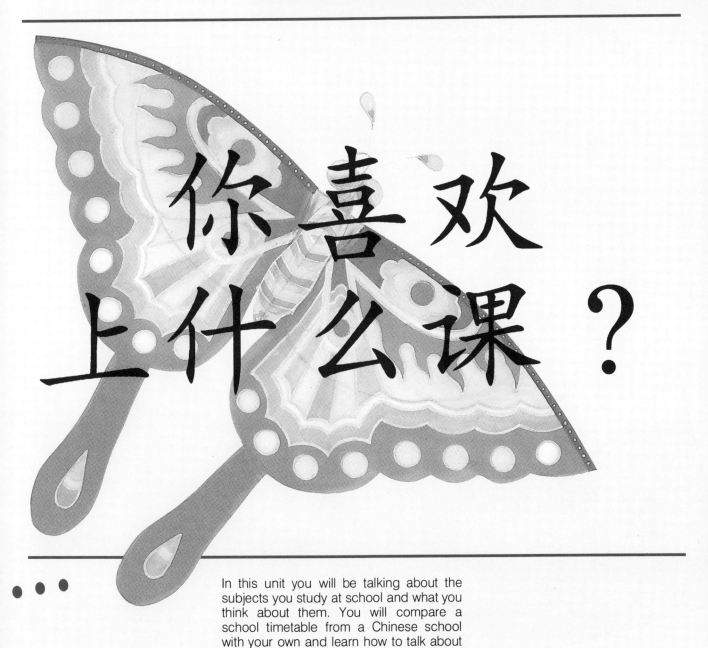

你喜欢上什么课？

In this unit you will be talking about the subjects you study at school and what you think about them. You will compare a school timetable from a Chinese school with your own and learn how to talk about how long you spend doing various activities each week. You will also learn how to talk about exams!

Schools in China

Schools in China are co-educational and practically all are run by the state. A typical secondary school in the cities would have about 1000 students. The curriculum is divided into junior secondary school (初中 *chūzhōng*) and senior secondary school (高中 *gāozhōng*) with three years of schooling each.

There are usually about 50 students in each class, with a class teacher in charge (班主任 *bānzhǔrèn*). The class is divided into groups (usually those students sitting in the same row). Each group elects its group leader. A class prefect and students in charge of education, cultural and sport activities, hygiene and so on are elected by the whole class to form a class committee. There are also subject representatives who assist teachers in collecting and distributing homework and, in general, serve as a liaison between the students and the subject teachers. Every student is thus encouraged to take part in the running of the day-to-day affairs of the class.

Each class has its own classroom — a 'home base' which is the responsibility of all the students belonging to that class to look after. They take great pride in decorating the classroom, writing for the 'wall newspaper' to report on events and happenings, students who have set a good example and so on. The groups take turns in keeping the classroom and its surroundings clean and tidy by sweeping the floor and arranging the furniture at the end of each school day.

Students are generally required to wear school uniforms during school hours. High school students share a code of conduct and each student is expected to be a 'three-good student' (三好学生 *sān hǎo xuéshēng**).

Physical punishment is prohibited, wrong-doing being rectified by counselling, criticism and self-criticism sessions. For serious and repeated offenders, disciplinary measures include a record of demerit, suspension or, in extreme cases, expulsion from the school.

All students enjoy concessions when they travel or go to the movies, exhibitions and so on.

* The 'three goods' are 身体好，学习好，工作好 (*shēntǐ hǎo, xuéxí hǎo, gōngzuò hǎo*), i.e. good health, good in studies and good at work (participation in the affairs of the group).

4.1 Counting from 100 to 9999

● 一百到九千九百九十九
(Yībǎi dào jiǔqiān jiǔbǎi jiǔshí jiǔ)

千 百 十 (个)
qiān bǎi shí (gè)

```
        1
     1  0
  1  0  0
1  0  0  0
```

三千四百二十一、
三千四百二十二、
三千四百二十三、
......

Here's how we count from 100 to 9999:

100	一百	yī**bǎi**
101	一百〇一	yībǎi líng yī
102	一百〇二	yībǎi líng èr
111	一百一十一	yībǎi yīshíyī
112	一百一十二	yībǎi yīshí'èr
200	二百	èrbǎi
999	九百九十九	jiǔbǎi jiǔshí jiǔ
1000	一千	yī**qiān**
1001	一千〇一	yīqiān líng yī
1018	一千〇一十八	yīqiān líng yīshíbā
1300	一千三百	yīqiān sānbǎi
9999	九千九百九十九	jiǔqiān jiǔbǎi jiǔshí jiǔ

Notes

1. 个 *gè*, 十 *shí*, 百 *bǎi*, 千 *qiān* represents 'unit', 'tens', 'hundreds' and 'thousands'.

2. 101 — The character 零 *líng* (meaning 'zero') is commonly written as 'O' in numbers. Remember that:
    a) *Líng* is usually *not* read out when it appears *at the end* of a figure.
    b) *Líng* is read out when it appears in a year, room number, telephone number and so on. For example:

        2001 nián   èr-líng-líng-yī nián
        402 hào fángjiān   sì-líng-èr hào fángjiān
        275–7030   èr-qī-wǔ-qī-líng-sān-líng

    c) *Líng* is read out when one or more zeroes appear *in the middle* of a figure. For example:

         306   sānbǎi líng liù
        3006   sānqiān líng liù
        3060   sānqiān líng liùshí

3. 112 — Note that we say *yībǎi yīshí'èr* (cf. *yībǎi èrshí'èr, yībǎi sānshí'èr* and so on).

该你了! →
Maths bee →

LEARN TO READ   page 150

LEARN TO WRITE   **Lesson 16**   page 166

该你了!

How would you say the following?
200   600   430   583   709
7000   2200   3450
6842   5007   4032

Maths bee

You can practise your numbers by doing some sums. To express addition you use 加 (*jiā*) meaning 'add', and 减 (*jiǎn*) meaning 'minus'.

Addition
2 + 4 = ?   二加四是几?
2 + 4 = 6   二加四是六。

Subtraction
17 – 9 = ?   十七减九是多少?
17 – 9 = 8   十七减九是八。

4.2   Talking about school life

● 我上二年级 (Wǒ shàng èr niánjí)

1. 你 好!

我 是 王 华。我 住 北京。
huá

我 今年 十三 岁。

我 上 初中 二 年级。
chū   jí

我们 学校 有 一千 二百 多 个 学生，
qiān　bǎi

差 不 多 有 六十 个 老师。
chà

2. 我 叫 李 强。
lǐ qiáng

我 是 王 华 的 同学。
huá

我们 都 在 二 年级 三 班。
jí

我们 的 班主任 是 李 老师。
bānzhǔrèn　lǐ

3. 我 是 丁 丽美。
dīng lìměi

我 和 王 华、李 强 同班。
huá lǐ qiáng bān

我们 班 一共 有 四十八 个 学生。
bān gōng

二十三 个 男生，

二十五 个 女生。

4 你们 好！我 是 林 英。
　　　　　　　　　　yīng

我 是 丁 丽 美 的 好 朋 友。
　　　dīng　lìměi

我 每 天 早 上 七 点 上 学，
八 点 半 上 课。
上 午 上 四 节 课，
　　　　　　jié

下 午 有 时 候 上 一 节，
　　　　　　　　　　jié

有 时 候 上 两 节。
　　　　　jié

我 们 每 天 下 午 五 点 半 放 学
回 家。

Find the Chinese →

Approximately 📼

When you want to express an approximate number or amount, you can use the approximate number indicators *duō* (多), or *jǐ* (几). For example:

10	**duō**	běn shū	*10 or more books*
10	**jǐ**	pǐ mǎ	*10 or more horses*
20	**duō**	gè xuésheng	*20-odd students*
120	**duō**	jiàn chènshān	*120-odd shirts*
1000	**duō**	gè rén	*over 1000 people*

Note that *duō* (多) shows the remainder of a figure, and in the above examples appears immediately after the number which may be '10', or amounts in the tens, hundreds, thousands and so on. It is not used with other numbers. For example, you do *not* say '13 *duō*' or '125 *duō*'.

Jǐ (几) is used to indicate an unspecified number smaller than 10. As with *duō*, you do *not* say '13 *jǐ*', or '135 *jǐ*'.

Find the Chinese

We finish school and go home every day at 5.30.
There are over 1200 students at our school.
We are both in Form 2C.
Sometimes we have one class in the afternoon and sometimes we have two.
I'm in the same class as Wang Hua and Li Qiang.
23 male students and 25 female students.
We have four classes in the morning.

Match up

1000 duō zhī yáng
bú dào 75 tiáo yú
10 jǐ zhī niǎo
chà bù duō 10 zhī niǎo
chà bù duō 75 tiáo yú
bú dào 1000 zhī yáng
750 duō tiáo yú

about 10 birds
less than 1000 sheep
less than 75 fish
10 or more birds
over 750 fish
about 75 fish
over 1000 sheep

You can also use *chà bù duō* (差不多) or *bú dào* (不到) to express approximate numbers. For example:

chà bù duō   20   běn shū   *about 20 books*
                 125 liàng qìchē   *about 125 cars*

bú dào   15   gè rén   *fewer than 15 people*
                 99   liàng zìxíngchē *fewer than 99 bicycles*
                 1500 zhī niǎo   *fewer than 1500 birds*

Match up   →   page 122
怎么说？ →
想一想 →
你听懂了吗？ →
Know your school →

LEARN TO READ   page 151

LEARN TO WRITE   Lesson 17   page 167

怎么说？

How would you express the following?

1. a) more than 2000 students
    b) fewer than 25 people
    c) more than 100 teachers
    d) fewer than 30 months
    e) over 70 bicycles
    f) about 20 weeks
    g) about 300 horses

2. a) I'm in the same class as David and Anna.
    b) I'm in the same class as Li Hua.
    c) Mary and I are both in Form 2B.
    d) David and Wang Yun are both in Form 3E.

3. Now that you can express approximate numbers and talk about who is in the same class as yourself, make five statements that are *true* about your own school and/or class.

想一想

Work in pairs. Ask each other these questions about Wang Hua's school.

1. *Wáng Huá de xuéxiào yǒu duōshao gè xuésheng?*
2. *Lǐ Qiáng shàng jǐ niánjí? Něige bān?*
3. *Shéi hé shéi tóngbān?*
4. *Tāmen bān yǒu duōshao gè xuésheng? Tāmen dōu shì nánshēng ma?*
5. *Tāmen de bānzhǔrèn shì shéi?*
6. *Tāmen jǐ diǎn shàngkè, jǐ diǎn fàngxué?*

Which of you answered most questions correctly?

你听懂了吗？

True or false?

1. a) The boy's school was a smaller school than the girl's.
    b) The boy's school was bigger than the girl's.

2. a) The girl attends a girls' school.
    b) She attends a coeducational school.

3. a) There are 800 students at the girl's school.
    b) There could possibly be more than 800 students at her school.
    c) There are not fewer than 800 students at her school.

4. a) There could possibly be 280 students at the boy's school.
    b) There are only 200 students at the boy's school.

Know your school

Can you answer these questions about your school?

1. *Nǐ shì něige xuéxiào de?* or
    Nǐ shàng něige xuéxiào?
    Nǐ shàng jǐ niánjí?
    Nǐ zài něige bān?
    Nǐmen de bānzhǔrèn shì shéi?

2. *Nǐmen de xiàozhǎng* shì shéi?*
    Shéi shì fùxiàozhǎng?**

3. *Nǐmen xuéxiào yǒu duōshao gè xuésheng?*
    Nǐmen xuéxiào yǒu jǐ gè niánjí?

4. *Nǐmen niánjí yǒu jǐ gè bān?*

5. *Nǐmen bān yǒu duōshao gè xuésheng?*
    Nǐmen bān yǒu duōshao gè nánshēng?
    Nǐmen bān yǒu duōshao gè nǔshēng?

    * *Xiàozhǎng* (校长) means 'school principal'.

    ** *Fùxiàozhǎng* (副校长) means 'deputy school principal'.

4.3 Asking permission and telling people what or what not to do

● 我可以进来吗？ (Wǒ kěyǐ jìnlai ma?)

> 我 可以 进来 吗？
>
> — 可以，请 进。
>
> 我 可以 走 了 吗？
>
> — 你 可以 走 了。
>
> 我 可以 看 电视 吗？
>
> — 现在 不 可以 看 电视。
>
> 我们 可以 在 这儿 吃 东西 吗？
>
> — 不行。

Notes:

1. *Wǒ kěyǐ jìnlai ma?* — 'May I come in?' *Kěyǐ…ma?* (可以……吗?) is used here to ask for permission.

2. *Bùxíng* — *Bùxíng* (不行) means 'No, you can't' and is an expression that always stands on its own, even when it is part of a longer sentence. For example:

   Wǒ xiànzài kěyǐ qù dǎ qiú ma?
   — *Bùxíng.*

   Wǒ kěyǐ gěi tā dǎ diànhuà ma?
   — *Bùxíng, tā jīntiān méiyǒu kòngr.*

   To say, for example, 'You may not (do something)', *bù kěyǐ* (不可以) is used, as in the sentence *Xiànzài bù kěyǐ kàn diànshì.*

● 不许迟到 *(Bùxǔ chídào)*

老师： 你 今天 怎么 迟到 了？
　　　　　　　　　　 chídào

小明： 我 的 表 停 了。
　　　　　　　　 tíng

老师： 明天 不许 再 迟到 了。
　　　　　　 xǔ　　　 chídào

小明： 好。

你们 不许
　　　 xǔ
在 这儿 骑 自行车！
　　　　 qí

不许
　 xǔ
在 这儿 停车！
　　　　 tíng

请勿 吸烟
QǏNG WÙ　XĪYĀN

不许 吸烟！
 xǔ　 xīyān

Notes:

Míngtiān bùxǔ zài chídào le — *Bùxǔ...* (不许……) indicates prohibition, i.e. that one is not allowed, or permitted to do something. *Bùxǔ* (不许) is more formal than *bù kěyǐ* (不可以), and is more often used with reference to rules and regulations (as in the sentences above).

你该锻炼身体了！ 📼
(Nǐ gāi duànliàn shēntǐ le!)

你们 不要 吵 了！
chǎo

不要 在 这儿 打 球！

你 该 收拾 房间 了！
gāi   shōushi

你 该 锻炼 身体 了！
gāi   duànliàn

不要 看 了！
去 睡觉！

Notes:

1. *Nǐmen búyào chǎo le!* — When we are telling someone not to do something *búyào . . .* （不要……）meaning 'must not', 'should not' or 'do not' is often used.
2. *Nǐ gāi shōushi fángjiān le!* — To tell someone that he or she must or should do something, *gāi* (该) is often used.
3. *Qù shuìjiào!* — When it is more in the nature of a curt order, brevity is required and the subject and *gāi* are usually left out. For example:

   Qù shuìjiào!
   Zuò zuòyè!

Find the Chinese →
你听懂了吗? →
怎么说? → page 127

Find the Chinese

Stop that noise!/ Stop squabbling!
Why are you late today?
You should be in bed!/ Go to bed!
Stop watching (television)!
Don't play ball games here!
Is it all right to eat here?
My watch stopped.
No smoking.
You should take some exercise!
No parking (allowed here).
Don't be late again tomorrow.
May I go?

你听懂了吗? 📼

1. True or false?
   a) The incident happened during a break.
   b) It happened during class.

2. The boys were playing in the classroom. True or false?

3. Why did the two boys finally agree to the girls' request?

Grounded

You're in trouble with your parents for getting very bad marks in your tests. They are very cross with you and tell you what you must do (*Nǐ gāi . . . le!*) and what you may not do (*Bùxǔ . . .*) in the coming week. Which of the following do they tell you that you must do and which do they tell you that you may not do?

qù kàn diànyǐng	gěi péngyou dǎ diànhuà
shǎo kàn diànshì	chūmén zhǎo péngyou
měi tiān zuò zuòyè!	wánr diànzǐ yóuxì
9 diǎn bàn shuìjiào!	duō fùxí gōngkè
cānjiā péngyou de shēngrìhuì	

● 帮朋友看孩子

(Bāng péngyou kān háizi)

You are baby-sitting some children you know. What will you say to them?

yào	wánr diànhuà
búyào	zài fángjiān lǐ tī qiú
gāi	zài zhèr xiě zì
	chīfàn le
	gěi xiǎo māo chī jīnyú
	chuān shuìyī
	qù shuìjiào le
	dǎjià le

怎么说?

1. How would you ask someone's permission to do the following?
   a) eat something
   b) come in
   c) watch TV
   d) go to play a ball game
   e) phone a friend

2. How would you tell someone not to do the following?
   a) eat in the classroom
   b) watch TV
   c) play here

Role play

With a partner, make up a situation based on 'Grounded' or *'Bāng péng-you kān háizi'* and role-play it in front of the class.

Role play →

上课的时候不许说话！📼
(Shàngkè de shíhou bùxǔ shuōhuà!)

1. 丁 力：   这 道 题 怎么 做？
   dīng   tí

   陈 新：   小 点儿 声！
   chén xīn   shēng

   老师：   不要 说话！

   丁 力：   老师，我 可以 问……。
   dīng

   老师：   上课 的 时候 不许 说话！
                        xǔ

2. 李 强：   你们 的 班主任 是 谁？
   lǐ qiáng

   丁 力：   刘 老师。
   dīng   liú

   李 强：   刘 老师？哪个 刘 老师？
            是 男 的 还是 女 的？

   丁 力：   男 的，他 个子 挺 高，戴
            眼镜。

   李 强：   哦，我 知道 了！你们 喜欢
            他 吗？

   丁 力：   不 喜欢。大家 都 怕 他。

3. 李 强：   为 什么？

Find the Chinese

No talking!
How did you know?
Don't stare out the window.
Which Teacher Liu? Male or female?
No talking in class!
Who's your form teacher?
No lateness allowed.
He's too strict.
Not so loud!
He's quite tall and wears glasses.
Don't fiddle with your pencils.
What are you laughing at?
How do you do this question?

丁 力： 他 太 严格 了。
dīng　　　　　　yángé

他 说，上课 以前 要 预习，
　　　　　　　　　　　　yùxí

下课 以后 要 复习。
　　　　　　fùxí

上课 的 时候 不许 说话。
　　　　　　　　xǔ

李 强： 哈，哈，哈，……。
lǐ qiáng　hā　hā　hā

丁 力： 你 笑 什么？
dīng　　　xiào

李 强： 他 还 说 不许 玩儿 铅笔，
　　　　　　　　xǔ　　　qiān

不许 看 窗外，
xǔ　　　chuāng

不许 迟到，不许……。
xǔ　chídào　　xǔ

丁 力： 你 怎么 知道？
李 强： 他 去年 是 我们 的
班主任！

Find the Chinese → page 128

你听懂了吗？ 📼

1. True or false?
   a) i) The rule was that they were not to play basket-ball at all.
      ii) The rule was that they could play there at any time.
      iii) The rule was that they could play there only at certain times.
   b) i) They thought they had permission to play on that court.
      ii) The boys were deliberately flouting school rules.

2. True or false?
   a) The girl was off to attend classes.
   b) She was going to a tennis session.

3. Does the school have a dress code? If so, what do you know about it?

Crazy sentences

Work in small groups. Each person in the group thinks of three sentences — one each about an action they do before, after or during another action. Divide each sentence onto three slips of paper under the headings:

- Action 1 (for example, *Wǒ chīfàn . . .*)
- Time when (*yǐqián/yǐhòu/de shíhou*)
- Action 2 (for example, *. . . tīng yīnyuè*)

All the slips of paper are placed in a jumbled order in three piles according to the headings. Everyone in the group then takes it in turn to take one slip from each group and read out the resulting sentence. How many make sense?

● 什么时候？ (Shénme shíhou?)

Here's how you say 'when', 'before', or 'after' something happened. For example:

Nǐ	chīfàn	**de shíhou**	búyào kàn diànshì.
	shàngxué	**yǐqián**	yào chī zǎofàn.
	qǐchuáng	**yǐhòu**	yào duànliàn shēntǐ.

你听懂了吗？ → page 129
Crazy sentences → page 129

练一练 (Liàn yí liàn)

Work in pairs, telling each other what you do on a typical day. For example:

Wǒ qǐchuáng yǐhòu kàn diànshì.

or

Qǐchuáng yǐhòu wǒ kàn diànshì.

Here are some questions to help you.

Nǐ	qǐchuáng	**yǐhòu**	zuò shénme?
	chī zǎofàn	**de shíhou**	tīng yīnyuè ma?
	chī zǎofàn	**yǐhòu**	qù shàngxué ma?
	shàngkè	**de shíhou**	zuò shénme?
	xiàkè	**yǐhòu**	dǎ qiú ma?
	zuò gōnggòng qìchē	**de shíhou**	xǐhuan zuò shénme?
	fàngxué	**yǐqián**	zài xuéxiào zuò shénme?
	huí jiā	**yǐhòu**	zuò shénme?
	chī wǎnfàn	**yǐhòu**	chángcháng kàn diànshì ma?
	shuìjiào	**yǐqián**	kàn shū ma?

可以不可以？ →
开会了！ →

LEARN TO READ page 153

LEARN TO WRITE Lesson 18 page 168

可以不可以？

Work in pairs. A writes down a number from Set 1, while B writes down a number from Set 2. If it's A's turn to ask, B shows A his or her number. A will then have to put the two phrases together in a question asking for B's permission. B gives permission if the request is a reasonable one and A scores a point. If not, he or she scores zero.

Set 1
1. *Zài chuáng shàng*
2. *Zài qìchē lǐ*
3. *Zài jiàoshì lǐ*
4. *Zài cāochǎng shàng*
5. *Qí zìxíngchē de shíhou*
6. *Chīfàn de shíhou*

Set 2
1. *dǎ qiú*
2. *kàn diànshì*
3. *tiàowǔ*
4. *chàng gē*
5. *kàn shū*
6. *tīng yīnyuè*

开会了！ (Kāihuì le!)

Hold a meeting (开会) in your class where you jointly compose a list of 'Do's and Don'ts' for the classroom to hang on the wall.

4.4 Talking about school subjects

● 你喜欢上什么课？
(Nǐ xǐhuan shàng shénme kè?)

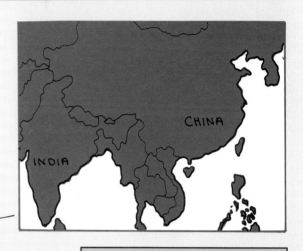

我 喜欢 上 历史课。
lì shǐ

历史课 很 有 意思。
lì shǐ   yìsi

我 想 去 中国 看看。
我 最 喜欢 地理课！
lǐ

我 觉得 外语 很 有 用。
我 喜欢 上 外语课。

我 很 喜欢 看 小说。
我 觉得 语文课 最 有
意思。
yìsi

我 喜欢 上 美术课。
měi shù

老师 说 我 画 画儿 画 得 很 好。
huà huà

你们 看，我 画 得 好 吗？
huà

Your subjects

Here are some other subjects you might be doing:

物理　wùlǐ　*Physics*
化学　huàxué　*Chemistry*
科学　kēxué　*Science*
手工艺　shǒugōngyì　*Manual Arts*
绘图　huìtú　*Graphics*
英语　Yīngyǔ　*English*
经济　jīngjì　*Economics*
商业原理　shāngyè yuánlǐ　*Business Principles*
生物　shēngwù　*Biology*
品德教育　pǐndé jiàoyù　*Citizenship Education*
家政　jiāzhèng　*Home Economics*
语言和戏剧　yǔyán hé xìjù　*Speech and Drama*
生理卫生和体育　shēnglǐ wèishēng hé tǐyù　*Health and Physical Education*
宗教教育　zōngjiào jiàoyù　*Religious Education*

我 最 喜欢 上 科学课 了！
kē

我 最 讨厌 数学。
tǎoyàn   shù

我 觉得 数学 太 难 学 了！
shù

我 喜欢 上 体育课。
我 打 球 打 得 非常 好！
我 是 球迷！
mí

难不难？ →
该你了 →
猜一猜 →

你觉得怎么样？

What do you think of the subjects you do at school? Here are some comments that you might make about the subjects you do.

Wǒ juéde kēxué zuì yǒu yòng.

lìshǐ

dìlǐ   méiyǒu yòng

měishù   hěn yǒu yìsi

wùlǐ   méiyǒu yìsi

wàiyǔ   tài nán xué le

tǐyù

shùxué   hěn róngyì

yǔwén

难不难？

难学 means 'difficult to study'.
Its opposite, 'easy to study', is 容易 学 *róngyì xué*.

1. How would you say the following?
    a) Physics is difficult (to study).
    b) Biology is easy (to study).
    c) Foreign languages are easy (to study).
    d) History is too difficult!

2. What do you think the speaker is saying or asking in the following?
    a) *Tā de jiā hǎo zhǎo.*
    b) *Zhège cí hěn nán jì.*
    c) *Zhège chéngxù hěn róngyì yòng.*
    d) *Wǒ tīngshuō Hànzì nán xiě nán jì. Nǐ shuō ne?*

该你了 (Gāi nǐ le!)

Work in pairs. Take it in turns to tell each other which subject:
*   you find most interesting
*   is your favourite
*   is your least favourite
*   you think is most useful
*   you find easiest to study
*   you find most boring
*   you find most difficult

猜一猜

Take it in turns to mime in front of the class a subject you are studying. Use body language to convey what you think of the subject. The rest of the class must:
*   guess what the subject is
*   guess how you feel about it

● 说汉语〔一〕

1. A: 我们 今天 有 汉语课 吗?

   B: 有。

   A: 是 上 新 课 还是 复习 旧 课?
      　　　　xīn　　　　　　　fùxí　jiù

   B: 上 新 课。
      　　xīn

2. A: 你 今年 还 上 音乐课 吗?
   B: 不 上 了。你 呢?
   A: 我 还 上。我 喜欢 音乐。

3. B: 你 明年 想 上 几 门 课?
      　　　　　　　　　mén

   A: 六 门。语文、数学、历史、生物、
      mén　　　　　shù　　lìshǐ

      化学 和 外语,你 呢?
      huà

      你 想 上 什么 课?
   B: 我 还 没有 想 好 呢。

4. A: 你 的 物理 作业 做 了 吗?
      　　　wùlǐ

   B: 还 没有,你 呢?
   A: 我 做完 了。
      　　　wán

5. A: 哎哟，怎么 办 呢？
      āiyō

   B: 怎么 啦？

   A: 昨天 的 数学 练习
            shù   liànxí

      我 还 不 会 做 呢！

   B: 你 复习 了 吗？
          fùxí

   A: 复习 了，可是 我 还 不 懂！
      fùxí

   B: 别 着急，我 帮 你。
      bié   zháojí

      来，咱们 一起 复习，好 吗？
                      fùxí

   A: 好！

Notes:

1. *Bié zháojí* — *Bié* (别) is another way of saying *búyào* (不要) meaning 'don't (do something)'. More examples:

    Bié shuōhuà!
    Qǐng nǐmen bié zài zhèr dǎ qiú, hǎo ma?

2. *Wǒ zuòwán le* — *Zuòwán* is made up of the verb *zuò* (to do) and the adjective *wán* (finish). *Wán* indicates the result of the action *zuò*, i.e. 'I have *finished* doing it', and is called a **resultative complement.**

VERB	+	RESULTATIVE COMPLEMENT (adjective or verb)
zuò		*wán*
xiǎng		*hǎo* (indicating completion)
chuān		*shàng* (indicating that the clothing is 'on')
kàn		*jiàn* (indicating that one has 'seen')
jiè		*gěi* (indicating to give or lend to someone)

Find the Chinese

Are you still doing Music this year?
I've dropped it./No, I'm not.
What's the matter?
I haven't quite decided yet.
I've done it.
Are we having a new lesson or are
  we having revision?
Oh dear, what shall I do?
yesterday's Maths exercises.
Did you revise it?
Do we have Chinese today?
Don't worry, I'll help you.
Let's do it together.

你听懂了吗？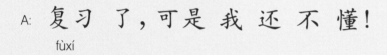

1. True or false?
    a) The boy has decided:
        i)   To do the same subjects
             next year.
        ii) To drop Economics for
             Biology.
        iii) To drop Biology for
             Economics.
    b) i)   The girl is also going to
             change her subjects.
        ii) The girl is doing the
             same subjects as this
             year.

2. a) True or false?
        i)   The boy thinks Chemis-
             try is a difficult subject.
        ii) He thinks Chemistry is
             not too difficult a sub-
             ject.
        iii) The girl agrees that it is
             a difficult subject.
        iv) She does not agree.
    b) What did they decide to do?

Note that resultative complements generally indicate that the action *has already happened*.

Méiyǒu (没有) is used to negate a verb with a resultative complement. For example,

*Tā **méiyǒu** kànjiàn wǒ.*
*Wǒ **méiyǒu** xiǎnghǎo.*
*Wǒ hái **méiyǒu** zuòwán zuòyè ne!*

Find the Chinese → page 134
你听懂了吗? → page 134
调查一下儿 →

LEARN TO READ page 155

LEARN TO WRITE **Lesson 19** page 169

调查一下儿

The class organises a survey (调查 *diàochá*) to find out which subjects members of the class are planning to do in Senior. Questions can be asked such as:

- *Nǐ gāozhōng shàng jǐ mén kè?*
- *Nǐ hái shàng Hànyǔ ma?*
- *Nǐ xiǎng shàng shénme kè?*

Before the survey, write down your predictions of which subjects you think will be most popular in Senior among your classmates. After the results of the survey are collated, see how many you got right!

4.5 Talking about your timetable

我的课程表 (Wǒ de kèchéngbiǎo)

Chinese school children attend classes from Monday to Saturday each week. A school day usually begins at around 7.30 and ends at about 5.00 in the afternoon.

你们 好!
我 是 林 英。
我 今年 十三 岁。
我 上 初中。
这 是 我们 初二 三班 的 课程表。

chéng

	星期一	星期二	星期三	星期四	星期五	星期六
7.30–7.50	早 自 习					
8.00–8.45	数学	语文	英语	数学	语文	英语
8.55–9.40	数学	数学	英语	英语	语文	语文
9.40–10.10	课 间 操					
10.10–10.55	语文	英语	数学	语文	政治 zhèngzhì	数学
11.05–11.50	体育	政治 zhèngzhì	语文	历史	数学	音乐
11.50–2.00	午 饭					
2.00–2.45	英语	音乐	校会	美术 měishù	英语	
2.55–3.40	地理 lǐ	历史	体育	地理 lǐ	自习	
4.00–5.30	课 外 活 动 huó					

今 天 是 星 期 一。

我 们 上 午 上 四 节 课，

下 午 上 两 节。

Find the Chinese

Straight after Music we have History.
Second period is Maths too.
We have Maths first period on Mondays.
After classes we have extra-curricular activities.

我们 星期一 上午
第一 节 课 是 数学，
dì

第二 节 课 也 是 数学，
dì

第三 节 课 是 语文，

第四 节 课 是 体育。

星期二 下午 从 2.00 到 2.45 上
cóng   dào

音乐课。上完 音乐课 就 上 历史课。
wán

下了 课 以后 有 课外 活动。
huó

Find the Chinese → page 136
你听懂了吗？ →
该你了！ →
Same or different? →

你听懂了吗？ 🔊

Listen carefully to the dialogues and statements about the time-table on page 136 and say whether the responses or comments are correct or not and why.

该你了！ (Gāi nǐ le!)

It's a Thursday. Look at the time-table and answer these questions.

1. *Tóngxuémen shàngwán shù-xuékè yǐhòu shàng shénme kè?*

2. *Tāmen shàngle dì jǐ jié kè yǐhòu yǒu kèwài huódòng?*

3. *Kèjiāncāo yǐqián shì wàiyǔkè ma?*

4. *Chīle wǔfàn yǐhòu, tāmen shàng shénme kè?*

Same or different?

Look carefully at Lin Ying's time-table and then write down a list of statements about it under two headings. One heading for the things that are the same (一样 *Yíyàng*) as your school timetable and one heading for the things that are different (不一样 *Bù yíyàng*). For example, under the heading 一样 (*Yíyàng*) you could write statements such as:

她每天上午上四节课。
她每天上一节语文课。

and under the heading 不一样 (*Bù yíyàng*) you could write statements such as:

每天下了课以后是课外活动。
每星期她上两节政治课。
他们课间做课间操。

You can work with a partner, but remember to discuss everything in Chinese!

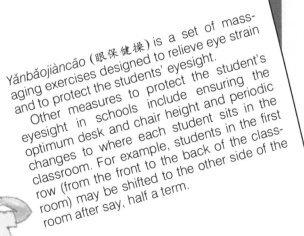

Yǎnbǎojiàncāo (眼保健操) is a set of mass-aging exercises designed to relieve eye strain and to protect the students' eyesight.

Other measures to protect the student's eyesight in schools include ensuring the optimum desk and chair height and periodic changes to where each student sits in the classroom. For example, students in the first row (from the front to the back of the class-room) may be shifted to the other side of the room after say, half a term.

说汉语（二） 📼

琳达： 借用 一下儿 你 的 汉语
líndá

课本，好 吗？

大卫： 不行，我 上午 要 用。
wèi

琳达： 你们 下 一 节 是 汉语课 吗？

大卫： 不 是，是 地理课，
lǐ

然后 才 是 汉语课。
rán

琳达： 哦，我们 下 一 节 是 汉语课。

我 可以 先 用 你 的 课本 吗？
xiān

大卫： 行。下 了 课 就 还 我。

琳达： 一定！
dìng

大卫： 别 忘 了！
bié

琳达： 放心 吧！
xīn

Find the Chinese

Don't worry!
No, we have Geography first, then we have Chinese.
Definitely!
Could I use your textbook first?
Could I borrow your Chinese text-book for a bit?
Don't forget!
Do you have Chinese next (class)?
Give it back to me straight after class.
Sorry, I need it this morning.
OK.

怎么说？

1. When David tells Linda 'Xiàle kè jiù huán wǒ', he uses the word jiù to stress that she should return the book immediately after she has finished class. How would you tell someone the following?
   a) to go and see Mr Smith straight after class
   b) to telephone you right after the Maths class
   c) that you will go home directly after going to the office
   d) that you are going to sleep straight after dinner

2. When David tells Linda '(Xià yī jié) shì dìlǐkè, ránhòu cái shì Hànyǔkè', he uses cái to indicate or emphasise that it is only after they have had Geography that they will have Chinese. How would you tell someone the following?
   a) that you will not go home until you have finished your Chinese homework
   b) that last night you did not go to bed until 11.30 pm

Notes:

Bú shì, shì dìlǐkè, ránhòu cái shì Hànyǔkè — *Cái* (才) is an adverb that has the sense of 'then and only then'. More examples:

Wǒ chīwán fàn cái huí jiā. I did not go home until I'd finished the meal.
Tā zuòwán zuòyè yǐhòu cái qù shuìjiào.
　　She did not go to bed until she'd finished her homework.
Tā 11 diǎn cái huí jiā. He did not return home until 11 o'clock.

Note that when time is mentioned, as in the last example, *cái* implies 'lateness'.

Find the Chinese → page 138
怎么说? → page 138

LEARN TO READ page 157

LEARN TO WRITE Lesson 20 page 170

4.6 Saying how long you do something for

● 小时和分钟 (Xiǎoshí hé fēnzhōng)

动动脑筋! (Dòngdong nǎojīn)

几 个 小时?

Look at the following expressions carefully.

半分钟
半年
半个月
半个小时
半天

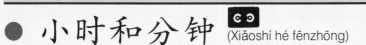

半 个 小时　一 个 小时　一 个 半 小时

What do they mean?
What do you notice about the use of the measure word 个?

多少 分钟?
zhōng

00:00:30　　00:02:00　　00:02:30

半 分 钟　　两 分 钟　　两 分 半 钟
zhōng　　　　　　　　　　　　　zhōng

动动脑筋! →
你听懂了吗? → page 140
听写 **Dictation** → page 140

她练习多长时间？(1) 💿

(Tā liànxí duō cháng shíjiān? 1)

To indicate how long one does something, all you have to do is to place the duration after the verb. You may place a 了 after the verb to indicate that the action is completed.

SUBJECT	VERB (了)	DURATION

For example:

她	练习（了） 玩儿（了）	多长时间？

她	练习（了） 睡（了） 玩儿（了）	一个小时。 十六个小时。 半个小时。

怎么说？ →

Here's what happens if the verb takes an object:

SUBJECT	VERB + OBJECT	VERB (了)	DURATION

For example:

她	上课 骑车 qí	上（了） 骑（了）	多长时间？
她	上课 骑车 qí	上（了） 骑（了）qí	四十五分钟。 二十分钟。

你听懂了吗？ 💿

Listen and say which is correct.

1. a) 4 hours
    b) 12 minutes
    c) 12 hours

2. a) 55 hours
    b) 55 minutes
    c) 50 minutes

3. a) 1 hour 52 minutes
    b) 7 hours 25 minutes
    c) 1 hour 25 minutes

4. a) 10 hours 4 minutes
    b) 4 hours 10 minutes
    c) 4 hours 4 minutes

5. a) 17 hours 11 minutes
    b) 11 hours 17 minutes

听写 Dictation

Work in pairs. Read all the above times back to your partner but in a jumbled order, jotting them down yourself as you do so. Your partner also writes the times down, in the order you say them. When you have finished, check your list against your partner's. Did your partner understand you correctly?
Now change over!

怎么说？

In reply to the question 'For how long did Mary practise?' you could say 'She practised for an hour' (*Tā liànxíle yí gè xiǎoshí*). How would you reply that she had practised for:

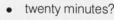

- two hours?
- half an hour?
- one and a half hours?
- twenty minutes?

As you can see, when the verb takes an object, the verb is repeated.

   VERB + OBJECT — VERB rpt. (le) — DURATION

Does this pattern remind you of another pattern you met earlier? (See Unit 1.)

多长时间？ →

多长时间？

Work in pairs. You and your partner ask each other how long yesterday you spent:

- watching television
- playing sport
- riding a bicycle/in a bus/in a car
- doing homework
- attending class

● 星期二的课 (Xīngqī'èr de kè)

1.

我们 星期二 上午 有
语文、数学、英语 和 政治。
                        zhèngzhì

下午 有 音乐 和 历史。

怎么说？

1. How would you tell someone that every day you spend:
   a) two hours doing your homework?
   b) ten minutes reviewing your schoolwork?
   c) nine hours sleeping?
   d) an hour playing sport?
   e) thirty-five minutes travelling by bus?

Hint:
You can frame your statements in two ways, either
   Wǒ měi tiān zuò zuòyè zuò liǎng gè xiǎoshí   or
   Wǒ měi tiān zuò liǎng gè xiǎoshí de zuòyè.

2. How would you tell someone that yesterday you spent:
   a) three and a half hours watching television?
   b) forty-five minutes playing sport?
   c) one hour tidying your room?
   d) half an hour reading a novel?
   e) fifty minutes playing video games?

	星期二
8.00–8.45	语文
8.55–9.40	数学
9.40–10.10	课间操
10.10–10.55	英语
11.05–11.50	政治 zhèngzhì
11.50–2.00	午饭
2.00–2.45	音乐
2.55–3.40	历史
4.00–5.30	课外 活动 huó

我们 每节 课 上
四十五 分钟。
         zhōng

我们 课间 休息
           xiūxi
十 分钟。
   zhōng

我们 中午 休息
          xiūxi
两 小时 零 十 分钟。
       líng   zhōng

2.

今天 下午 有 课外 活动。
huó

我 跑步 跑了 十五 分钟。
zhōng

我们 打 乒乓球
pīngpāng

打了 半 个 小时。

练一练

Ask your friend questions about how long these people have been doing these things:

跳舞 (20 minutes)
tiàowǔ

睡觉 (one morning)

玩儿 电子 游戏 (nearly an hour)
xì

做 健身操 (less than half an hour)

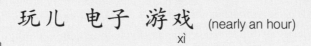

打 网球 (more than forty minutes)
wǎng

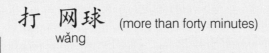

等 朋友 (about 10 minutes)

你听懂了吗? [cc]

1. a) Which would be more probable?
   i) Linda went overseas on a business trip.
   ii) She was on holiday on her own.
   iii) She was on holiday where her parents live.

   b) True or false?
   i) The man arrived just in time to meet her.
   ii) He had been waiting for some time.
   iii) He was late.

   c) True or false?
   i) There was a two-hour long stopover in Singapore.
   ii) It was more than two hours.
   iii) It was for one hour only.

2. a) True or false?
   i) The boy spent one hour at David's house.
   ii) He spent a whole day at David's house.
   iii) He spent a whole afternoon at David's house.

   b) True or false?
   i) The boy went to bed at 12.30.
   ii) He went to bed at 12.00.
   iii) He went to bed at 11.30.

   c) Could he go back to bed? Why or why not?

● 她练习多长时间？(2)

(Tā liànxí duō cháng shíjiān? 2)

When the verb takes on an object, here's another way of expressing how long you spend doing things.

SUBJECT	VERB (了)	DURATION	的 OBJECT
她	上（了）	五个小时	的 课。
他	骑（了） qí	二十分钟 zhōng	的 车。
他们	打（了）	半个小时	的 球。

More examples:

Tā	kàn(le)	sān gè xiǎoshí	de	diànshì.
Mǎlì	zuò(le)	bàn gè xiǎoshí	de	jiànshēncāo.
Nǐ	fùxí(le)	duō cháng shíjiān	de	Hànyǔ?

怎么说？ → page 141
你听懂了吗？ → page 142
Commuter survey →
你身体好吗？ →
Class profile → page 144

Commuter survey

1. Organise a survey in your class to find out how much time everyone spends travelling to and from school. Tabulate the results on a large graph and write statements that describe the length of time your class as a whole spends travelling. For example:

   Wǒmen bān de tóngxué měi tiān yígòng qí 12 xiǎoshí de chē.

2. Make your own personal graph of the time you spend commuting to and from school with statements written underneath to explain the graph. For example:

   Wǒ měi tiān zuò bàn gè xiǎoshí de huǒchē.

3. From the personal graphs of the class, find out the following information.
   a) Who spends the most time travelling each day?
   b) Who spends the shortest time?
   c) Which is the commonest means of travelling to and from school?
   d) Does anyone walk?

你身体好吗？
Fitness survey

1. Find out from members of your class:
   a) if they take exercise
   b) how often they exercise
   c) what form of exercise they take
   d) for how long they exercise

2. Collate the results of your surveys and declare who is the fittest person in the class!

● 说汉语（三）　📼

1.　彼得：　下了 课 你 有 事儿 吗?
　　　bǐ

　　安娜：　我们 音乐 小组 要 活动
　　　ānnà　　　　　　　zǔ　　huó

　　　　　　一 个 小时。有 事儿 吗?

　　彼得：　我 想 去 打 网球。你 去 吗?
　　　bǐ　　　　　　　　wǎng

　　安娜：　我 下午 四 点 以后 才 有
　　　ānnà

　　　　　　空儿。

　　彼得：　没 关系，我们 可以 四 点
　　　　　　　　guānxi

　　　　　　以后 去 打 球。

　　　　　　我 四 点 钟 来 找 你。
　　　　　　　　　　zhōng

　　安娜：　不，四 点 在 网球场 见。
　　　　　　　　　　　　wǎng

　　彼得：　好，再见!

2.　玛丽：　上午 上了 两 节
　　　mǎlì

　　　　　　数学， 两 节 语文。我 累死 了!
　　　　　　　　　　　　　　　lèisǐ

Class profile

1. Conduct a survey to find out who in your class each week:
   a) sleeps the most/least
   b) watches the most/least television
   c) spends the most/least time playing computer games?
   d) spends the most/least time reading novels
   e) spends the most/least time talking on the telephone

2. Graph the results and pin them on your class noticeboard with statements describing your findings. For example:

   XX měi gè xīngqī shuì 70 xiǎoshí de jiào. Tā shuì de zuì duō.

   XX měi gè xīngqī shuì 50 xiǎoshí de jiào. Tā shuì de zuì shǎo.

大卫: 没 关系，中午 你 可以
wèi   guānxi

休息 一 个 小时。
xiūxi

玛丽: 我 下午 还 有 课 呢!
mǎlì

大卫: 我 也 有 课。
wèi

玛丽: 放学 以后，我 还 要
mǎlì

学 一 个 小时 的 音乐，
还 要 去 找 朋友，
还 要 去 看 电影。

大卫: 你 真 是 个 大忙人儿!
wèi   máng

Find the Chinese

I'm exhausted!
I won't be free until after 4 o'clock.
I'm going to go and have a game of tennis.
Are you doing anything after classes?
You really are a Busy Bee!
No, I'll meet you on the court at 4 o'clock.
Our group has to practise for an hour.
Do you want to come?
You can rest for an hour at midday.
I also have to go and see some friends.
I'll come and get you at 4 o'clock.
I still have an hour of music practice.
I have classes this afternoon too!

我更忙!

Role-play a situation where two people are saying how busy they are, each implying that he or she is busier than the other.

Notes:

Wǒmen yīnyuè xiǎozǔ yào huódòng yí gè xiǎoshí — Yào (要) here has the sense of 'need to' or 'have to'.

Find the Chinese →
我更忙! →

LEARN TO READ page 159

LEARN TO WRITE Lesson 21 page 171

4.7   Talking about exams

● 考试了！ (Kǎoshì le!)

你们 今天 考试 吗？
　　　　　kǎo

考，考！
kǎo

你们 今天 考 什么？
　　　　kǎo

我 考 历史。
kǎo

他 一定 考 得 很 好。
　　dìng　kǎo

我 考 外语。
kǎo

看来，
他 复习 得 很 好。

我 考 物理。

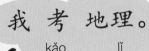

我 考 地理。
kǎo　　　　lǐ

他 还 不 会 呢！

我 考 数学。

他 没有 复习！

他 紧张 极 了！
jǐnzhāng　jí

● **你得了多少分？**
(Nǐ déle duōshao fēn?)

我 考了 98 分！
kǎo

他 外语
考 得 非常 好！
kǎo

她 及格 了。
jígé

我 得了 62 分。

他 不 及格。
jígé

我 数学 得了 20 分。

In Chinese schools, exam papers are generally marked out of 100. However, small tests （小测验 *xiǎo cèyàn*) are usually marked out of 5 points. This is graded as follows:	
五分	excellent
四分	good
三分	pass
两分	poor (fail)
一分	bad

谁考得好？ (Shéi kǎo de hǎo?)

Here are copies of Linda, Peter, Leigh and Jenny's exam papers. How did they do in the tests?

● **我怕考试！**  (Wǒ pà kǎoshì!)

1. 兰兰： 我 真 怕 考 得 不 好，你 呢？
lánlán   kǎo

建华： 我 不 怕。我 都 会 了。
jiànhuá

我 昨天 晚上 复习了 六 个 小时。

兰兰： 哎哟，你 昨天 晚上 几 点 睡觉？
āiyō

建华： 一 点 半。

兰兰： 那 你 不 困 吗？
lánlán   kùn

建华： 没 事 儿！
jiànhuá

2. 兰兰：考 得 怎么样？
　　　　kǎo

建华：不 怎么样！

兰兰：为 什么？

建华：我 太 累 了！
　　　　　　　lèi

考试 的 时候
kǎo

我 想 睡觉！

兰兰：没 关系，能 及格 就 行。
　　　　　　guānxi　　　jígé

Find the Chinese →
你听懂了吗? →

● 说汉语（四）

1. 马丁：咱们 今天 下午 去 滑冰，
　　　　mǎdīng　　　　　　　　　　huábīng

好 吗？

珍妮：我 今天 没 空儿，
zhēnnī

我们 明天 有 历史 测验。
　　　　　　　　　　cèyàn

我 得 复习 功课。

马丁：历史 挺 容易 的。

Find the Chinese

What time did you go to bed?
No problem!
I'm really scared of doing badly in this exam.
As long as you pass that'll do.
How did you go?
I spent 6 hours swotting last night.
So aren't you tired?
I was too sleepy.
Not so well.
I know how to do everything.

你听懂了吗?

1. True or false?
   a) i) The boy and girl are classmates.
   ii) They are in the same grade.
   iii) They are not in the same grade.
   b) i) The boy was sitting for the exam the following day.
   ii) He sat for the exam today.
   c) i) He was worried that he would not do well.
   ii) He was well prepared and confident.

2. a) True or false?
   i) The girls felt that the boy did well in the exam.
   ii) They felt that he should have done better.
   b) Which is more probable?
   i) The exam was easy.
   ii) The exam was too difficult.

珍妮: 你 会 就 容易, 我 还 不 会 呢!
zhēnnī

2. 劳拉: 怎么 啦?
láolā

彼得: 我 累死 了! 我们 刚才 考了
bǐ   lèisǐ   kǎo

一个 小时 的 数学。

劳拉: 我们 也 考 了 数学。
kǎo

你 考 得 怎么样?
kǎo

彼得: 还 可以, 你 呢?

劳拉: 我 觉得 考 得 不错。
kǎo

彼得: 第一 题 太 容易 了。
tí

劳拉: 是。

彼得: 你 得 多少?

劳拉: 0。

彼得: 0? 你 错了! 我 得 1。
第二 题 呢?
tí

劳拉: 我 想想, ……我 得 75。

彼得： 不 对！我 得74。
bǐ

劳拉： 哎哟，我们 快 去 问问
láolā   āiyō

老师 吧！

Notes:

Wǒmen míngtiān yǒu lìshǐ cèyàn — *Cèyàn* (测验) is a 'test', whereas a *kǎoshì* (考试) is a major exam. A short test (for example, a vocabulary test for the Unit) is called a *xiǎo cèyàn* (小测验).

Find the Chinese   →
Role play   →

LEARN TO READ   page 161

LEARN TO WRITE   **Lesson 22**   page 172

Find the Chinese

Let's ask the teacher.
What's the matter?
You're wrong.
I can't, we have an exam tomorrow.
Not bad.
I'm exhausted.
I think I went OK.
What exam do you have?
Question 1 was dead easy.
We've just had a one-hour maths test.
How did you go?
It's easy if you know it.
What answer did you get?
I have to revise.

Role play

Role-play Laura's and Peter's discussion with the Maths teacher.

学会认字

4.1

Before reading the text, listen to the recording and answer the questions.

Dialogue 1
True or false?
1. a) The girl was surprised that the boy's school had so many students.
    b) She was seeking confirmation of the number of students in the boy's school.
2. a) The boy also thinks that it is a rather big school.
    b) He thinks it is not very big.
3. a) The boy's school has twice as many students as the girl's.
    b) It had more than three times as many students.

Dialogue 2
True or false?
1. It's likely that the girl and the boy are in the same grade.
2. She is probably in a higher grade.
3. She is probably in a lower grade.

● 汉字表

				As in
千	qiān	*thousand*		一千
百	bǎi	*hundred*		二百

Text 〇つ

1. G: 你们学校学生多吗?

   B: 不少, 有一千四百个学生。

   G: 真的啊?! 老师呢?

   B: 有五十八个老师。

   G: 你们学校人真多!

   B: 你们呢?

   G: 我们学校有四百个学生。
   十二个老师。

   B: 哦, 你们学校真小!

2. G: 你到现在学了多少个汉字?

   B: 我们学了一百七十个汉字, 你们呢?

   G: 我们学了二百二十个。

4.2

Before reading the text, listen to the recording and answer the questions.

<u>Dialogue 1</u>
True or false?
1. The girl and the boy are schoolmates.
2. The school is co-educational.
3. There are about 600 female students in the school.

<u>Dialogue 2</u>
True or false?
1. The woman who is talking to the boy is over 40 years old.
2. The school the boy goes to is co-educational.
3. The principal of the school is over 40 years old.
4. The principal is a woman.
5. The principal was once the woman's teacher.

Narrative

True or false?

1. Wang Xing is in Grade 2 of high school.
2. There are seven grades in his high school.
3. He attends classes for five days a week.
4. Classes start at 8 o'clock.
5. He has time each day to play sports.

● 汉字表

			As in
〇	líng	zero (in figures)	二〇〇一年
象	xiàng	appearance; image	好象
级	jí	grade; level; rank	九年级
长	zhǎng	elder; senior	校长
班	bān	class; (work) shift	三班;同班;上班
初	chū	at the beginning of	初中
共	gòng	altogether, in all	一共
主	zhǔ	main; primary	班主任
任	rèn	official post; office	
节	jié	(measure word)	五节课

Text 📼

1. G: 你上哪个中学？

   B: 一〇四中。

   G: 你们学校有多少个学生？

   B: 一千二百多个学生。

   G: 有多少个男生，多少个女生？

   B: 好象是一半一半。

2. W: 你今年上几年级？

   B: 九年级。

   W: 你在哪个学校上学？

B: 男四中。

W: 男四中? 谁是你们的校长?

B: 林华。

W: 林华? 是男的吗?

B: 是。

W: 他多大?

B: 四十多岁。

W: 他戴眼镜吗?

B: 戴。

W: 哦, 我认识他, 他是我大学同班同学。

3. 我叫王星, 我今年上初中二年级。我们年级一共有七个班。我在三班。我们的班主任是谢明老师。

我们一个星期上六天课。每个星期一共有三十四节课, 有时候一天上五节课, 有时候上六节。

我每天早上七点上学, 八点上课。上午上四节课, 下午有时候上一节课, 有时候上两节课。我们下午三点四十分下课。下了课, 我常常去球场打球, 有时候跑跑步, 四点回家。

动动脑筋
(Dòngdong nǎojīn)

1. Which is correct?

   高班同学

   is someone in your school who is
   a) in a higher grade
   b) a tall student in your class

2. Why would you like to own a car that is described as

   高级?

3. When do you think this is?

   月初
   年初

4.3

Before reading the text, listen to the recording and answer the questions.

Dialogue 1
True or false?

1. The boy and girl had difficulty stopping their car.
2. They were trying to find a parking spot.
3. They could not read the sign from where they were.
4. They found a parking spot across the road.

Dialogue 2

True or false?
1. The boy was planning to visit a friend.
2. He said he would be coming back late.
3. His mother was worried that he would be out too late.
4. The boy said he would be home by 9.00.

Dialogue 3

True or false?
1. The argument was about the boy's homework.
2. The girl was watching TV.
3. The boy was doing his homework in the lounge.
4. He could have done his homework that afternoon.

● 汉字表

			As in
停	tíng	to stop	停车
许	xǔ	to allow; permit	不许
声	shēng	sound; voice	小点儿声
吵	chǎo	quarrel; make a noise	吵什么？

Text

1. G: 可以在这儿停车吗？
   B: 不知道，我去看看。

   ……

   不行，不可以在这儿停车。
   G: 那我们在哪儿停车呢？
   B: 在那边儿，…… 对面。

2. B: 妈，我星期六晚上想去同学家里玩
   儿。可以吗？
   W: 可以。你几点回家？
   B: 九点多。

W: 好。不许太晚了！

3. 哥哥： 你小点儿声,好不好？
      我正在做作业呢！

   妹妹： 刚才一个下午,
      你怎么不做作业？

   哥哥： 我下午有事儿。

   妹妹： 有事儿？你就知道打球！

   妈妈： 你们吵什么？

   哥哥： 我正在做作业。她看电视。
      我让她小点儿声她不听！

   妹妹： 怕吵就不要在这儿做作业,
      去房间做！

   妈妈： 好了,好了,
      你小点儿声。
      你去你房间做作业。
      不许吵了！

动动脑筋

(Dòngdong nǎojīn)

Which of these happenings would you be most likely to enjoy?

停电
停课

4.4

Before reading the text, listen to the recording and answer the questions.

Dialogue 1
True or false?
1. The boy and the girl are classmates.
2. They have English lessons every Wednesday.
3. The teacher will be starting a new lesson today.

Narrative
True or false?
1. Xu Ying is in Grade 10.
2. She has to decide which five subjects she will do next year.
3. She thinks Maths is not necessarily a difficult subject.
4. She feels that the key to success in History is to read a lot and to remember what one has read.

● 汉字表

			As in
英	yīng	(abbrev. of 英国 England)	英语；英文
新	xīn	new	新课
数	shù	number	数学
历	lì	to undergo	历史
史	shǐ	history	
门	mén	(measure word); door, gate	两门课，大门
练	liàn	to practise; train	练习
习	xí	to practise; review	

Text 📼

1. G: 今天是星期三还是星期四？

   B: 今天是星期三。

   G: 下午是英语课还是体育课？

   B: 英语。

   G: 是学新课吗？

   B: 是。

2.　　我叫许英，我明年上十一年级。明年我想上英语、数学、历史……，还有两门课，我还没有想好。

　　很多人说数学和历史很难，不容易学，我觉得也对也不对。我觉得学数学天天要做练习。练习做得多，你就不觉得难了。学历史也要多看，多记。看得多，记得多，就不觉得历史难学了。你说，我说得对不对？

问一问

Find out when your local Chinese community celebrate

新年

this year.

动动脑筋

(Dòngdong nǎojīn)

1. Where would you find this in a house?

   a) 前门

   b) 后门

2. To avoid going through the proper channels when they want something done, some people do this:

   走后门儿。

   What do you think it means?

3. If you wanted to ask someone a favour and that person said:

   没门儿!

   Would you be pleased?

4.5

Before reading the text, listen to the recording and answer the questions.

Dialogue 1
True or false?
1. The girl and the boy take their Chinese lessons together.
2. The third period for them is Chinese.
3. They are starting a new Chinese lesson today.
4. They arranged to meet before the Chinese lesson.

Dialogue 2
True or false?
1. The boy was looking forward to the weekend.
2. His best subjects were Maths and English.
3. He would not have any homework.
4. He was going to a movie during the weekend.
5. The girl had a lot of studying to do over the weekend.

● 汉字表

			As in
复	fù	*again*	复习
旧	jiù	*old; used; worn*	旧课；旧衣服
别	bié	*do not*	别高兴得太早了
第	dì	*(indicating ordinal number)*	第一节课
功	gōng	*skill*	功课
物	wù	*thing; matter*	生物

Text 🔊

1. G: 今天的汉语课是复习旧课还是学新课？

   B: 你忘了？
      老师说今天复习旧课。

   G: 哦，我记起来了，今天是复习！
      在哪个教室上课？

   B: 在八号教室上课。

   G: 第一、第二节你上什么课？

B: 我们在楼下上英语,你呢?

G: 我们在楼上。我们上数学。

B: 这样吧,第二节课以后我在楼下
等你。咱们一起去八号教室。

G: 好,一会儿见!

B: 再见!

2. G: 你今天怎么这么高兴?

B: 你忘了?今天是星期五。

G: 星期五怎么啦?

B: 是最后一天上课!
明天、后天我们不用上课了!
太好了!

G: 你别高兴得太早了。
我们今天还要上课呢!

B: 今天没什么,上午第一、第二节
课是数学;第三、第四节是英
语。这两门课我都学得很好,我
不怕。下午是自习,我可以复习
功课,做作业。你呢?

G: 我上午有数学、汉语和历史,下午
有生物。

B: 我星期六、星期日想去找朋友,看
电影。

G: 我没有空儿去玩儿。我星期六、
星期天得复习功课。

动动脑筋

(Dòngdong nǎojīn)

What is the state of something that is described as

半新不旧?

4.6

Before reading the text, listen to the recording and answer the questions.

<u>Dialogue</u>
True or false?
1. The conversation was about how difficult the exercises were.
2. The boy finished his exercises in less than half the time it took the girl.
3. The girl felt the exercises were difficult.
4. The boy made a few mistakes.

<u>Narrative</u>
True or false?
1. Mr Huang has been teaching Chinese for more than ten years.
2. He has just arrived in Australia.
3. He spends one to two hours each day trying to improve his English.
4. He does not spend any of his spare time with his students.
5. He is still teaching Chinese in Australia.

● 汉字表

			As in
完	wán	to finish; complete	做完练习
错	cuò	wrong; (resultative complement)	做错
教	jiāo	teach, instruct	教汉语
休	xiū	to stop, cease	休息
息	xī	to stop, cease	
然	rán	so; like that	然后
钟	zhōng	time measured in hours and minutes; clock	分钟
到	dào	arrive at; (resultative complement)	见到

Text 🔘

1. G: 今天的英语练习你做完了吗？

    B: 做完了。

    G: 你做得真快！

    B: 你呢？

G: 还没有。

B: 今天的练习很容易。
我半个小时就做完了。

G: 是吗？
我怎么觉得挺难的？

B: 我看看你的。……
哦，我都做错了！

G: 你做得太快了！

2.   黄老师是北京人。他在中国教了十年的汉语。两年以前他来澳大利亚，现在在我们学校教我们汉语。他每个星期教我们六个小时的汉语课。他教汉语教得非常好。我们大家都非常喜欢他。

      每天中午我们有一个小时的休息时间。黄老师常常和我们一起吃午饭。这样，大家可以练习说汉语。我们大家都很高兴。

      每天晚饭以后，黄老师看半个小时的电视，然后学一个小时的英语。睡觉以前还看二十分钟的英语小说。现在他的英语说得很好。

      黄老师上个星期回中国了。我明年要去中国，我想我会在北京再见到他。

动动脑筋
(Dòngdong nǎojīn)
Where would you expect to find a
休息室?

4.7

Before reading the text, listen to the recording and answer the questions.

Dialogue 1
True or false?
1. The boy was nervous because he did not know his work.
2. He had spent a lot of time preparing for the Biology test.
3. The girl was also faced with a test on the same day.
4. The girl tried to reassure him that he would do well in the test.

Dialogue 2
True or false?
1. The Biology test went quite well for the boy.
2. The Biology questions were not very difficult.
3. The History questions were also not very difficult.
4. The History test went on for two hours.

● 汉字表

			As in
考	kǎo	to give or take an examination	考什么?
紧	jǐn	tight; taut	紧张
张	zhāng	to stretch; open	
定	dìng	to decide, fix, set	一定
题	tí	problem; topic	考试题
道	dào	(measure word)	六道题
及	jí	to reach, attain	及格
格	gé	standard	
关	guān	be concerned with	关系
系	xì	to be related to	

Text

1. G: 你们今天考什么?

   B: 生物,你呢?

G: 历史。

B: 我真怕考得不好。

G: 不要紧张。你复习了吗?

B: 复习了。我昨天复习了一个
下午,晚上还复习了两个小时。

G: 你都懂了吗?

B: 都懂了。

G: 那你怕什么? 不要紧张,
你一定会考得很好!

B: 谢谢。

2. G: 昨天的生物考试,你考得怎么
样?

B: 不错。昨天的考试题很容易,
我想我能得九十分。

G: 那太好了!

B: 你呢? 你的历史考得怎么样?

G: 不太好。我觉得我们的考试题太难
了。我们考了两个小时,我还有一
道题没有做完。

B: 没关系,能及格就行。

动动脑筋

(Dòngdong nǎojīn)

If a 新生 is a new student, who would this be?

考生

SUMMARY

(LTR stands for Learn to Read; LTW stands for Learn to Write)

4.1 Counting from 100 to 9999

Now you can:

count from 100 to 9999:
Yìbǎi líng èr　一百〇二
Jiǔqiān bābǎi wǔshíliù　九千八百五十六

Useful expression
Zhēn de ma?　真的吗?　*Is that so? Really?*

4.2 Talking about school life

Now you can:

say you are in the same class as someone:
Wǒ hé Wáng Huá, Lǐ Qiáng tóngbān.
我和王华、李强同班。
Wǒmen dōu zài èr niánjí sān bān.
我们都在二年级三班。

say approximately how many students or teachers are at your school:
Wǒmen zhōngxué yǒu yìqiān èrbǎi duō gè xuésheng.
我们中学有一千二百多个学生。
Chà bù duō yǒu liùshí gè lǎoshī.
差不多有六十个老师。

talk about your school routine:
Wǒ měi tiān zǎoshang qī diǎn shàngxué, bā diǎn bàn shàngkè.　我每天早上七点上学，八点半上课。
Shàngwǔ shàng sì jié kè, xiàwǔ yǒu shíhou shàng yì jié, yǒu shíhou shàng liǎng jié.　上午上四节课，下午有时候上一节，有时候上两节。
(LTR) Wǒmen yí gè xīngqī shàng liù tiān kè.
我们一个星期上六天课。
(LTR) Yǒu shíhou yì tiān shàng wǔ jié kè, yǒu shíhou shàng liù jié.　有时候一天上五节课，有时候上六节。

Useful expressions
(LTR) yíbàn yíbàn　一半一半　*half and half*
(LTR) yī líng sì zhōng　一〇四中　*No. 104 high school*
(LTR) tóngbān tóngxué　同班同学　*fellow students in same class; classmates*
(LTR) yì tiān　一天　*one day; a whole day*

4.3 Asking permission and telling people what or what not to do

Now you can:

ask permission to do something:
Wǒ kěyǐ jìnlai ma?　我可以进来吗?
Wǒ kěyǐ zǒu le ma?　我可以走了吗?

give or deny permission:
Kěyǐ.　可以。
Bù kěyǐ.　不可以。
Bùxíng.　不行。

say something is not allowed:
Bùxǔ zài zhèr tíng chē!　不许在这儿停车!
Bùxǔ xīyān!　不许吸烟!

tell someone to do something or not to do something:
Qù shuìjiào!　去睡觉!
Nǐ gāi shōushi fángjiān le!　你该收拾房间了!
Nǐmen búyào chǎo le!　你们不要吵了!
Búyào zài zhèr dǎ qiú!　不要在这儿打球!
Bùxǔ zài chídào le!　不许再迟到了!
Búyào kàn (diànshì) le.　不要看(电视)了。

say what you do before, after or during another activity:
Wǒ chī wǎnfàn yǐhòu chángcháng kàn diànshì.
我吃晚饭以后常常看电视。
Wǒ shuìjiào yǐqián kàn shū.　我睡觉以前看书。
Wǒ chī zǎofàn de shíhou tīng yīnyuè.
我吃早饭的时候听音乐。

Useful expressions

Nǐ xiào shénme?　你笑什么?　*What's funny? What are you laughing at?*

Xiǎo diǎnr shēng!　小点儿声!　*Be a bit quieter!*

(LTR) Bùxǔ tài wǎn le!　不许太晚了!　*Don't be too late (home)!*

(LTR) Nǐ jiù zhīdao dǎ qiú!　你就知道打球!　*All you care about is playing tennis (ball games)!*

(LTR) Gāngcái yí gè xiàwǔ　刚才一个下午　*the afternoon just passed*

(LTR) Nǐmen chǎo shénme?　你们吵什么?　*What are you quarrelling about?*

(LTR) Hǎo le, hǎo le.　好了,好了　*All right, all right. That's enough . . .*

4.4　Talking about school subjects

Now you can:

say what you think about the school subjects you are doing:

Wǒ juéde wàiyǔ hěn yǒu yòng.　我觉得外语很有用。

Wǒ zuì xǐhuan shàng shùxuékè le!
我最喜欢上数学课了!

Wǒ juéde yǔwénkè zuì yǒu yìsi.
我觉得语文课最有意思。

Wǒ zuì tǎoyàn shùxué. Wǒ juéde shùxué tài nán xué le!
我最讨厌数学。我觉得数学太难学了!

ask someone what subjects they are taking:

Nǐ jīnnián hái shàng yīnyuèkè ma?
你今年还上音乐课吗?

possible replies:

Bú shàng le.　不上了。

Wǒ hái shàng.　我还上。

Useful expressions

Wǒ zěnme bàn!　我怎么办!　*What shall I do? What's to be done?*

Bié zháojí.　别着急。　*Don't worry.*

Wǒ hái méiyǒu xiǎnghǎo.　我还没有想好。　*I haven't quite decided yet.*

Extra vocabulary
more school subjects　page 131

4.5　Talking about your timetable

Now you can:

describe your school timetable:

Dì-yī jié kè shì shùxué.　第一节课是数学。

Dì-sān jié kè shì yǔwén.　第三节课是语文。

Wǒmen xīngqī'èr xiàwǔ cóng 2.00 dào 2.45 shàng yīn-yuèkè.　我们星期二下午从2.00到2.45上音乐课。

Shàngwán yīnyuèkè jiù shàng lìshǐkè.
上完音乐课就上历史课。

Xiàle kè yǐhòu yǒu kèwài huódòng.
下了课以后有课外活动。

ask someone why they are so . . . :

(LTR) Nǐ jīntiān zěnme zhème gāoxìng?　你今天怎么这么高兴?　*How come you're so happy today?*

Useful expressions

Yídìng.　一定。　*Certainly.*

Xià yì jié (kè)　下一节 (课)　*next lesson*

Bié wàng le!　别忘了!　*Don't forget!*

Fàngxīn ba!　放心吧!　*Relax! Don't worry!*

(LTR) Xīngqīwǔ zěnme la?　星期五怎么啦?　*What about Friday?*

(LTR) Zuìhòu yì tiān shàngkè.　最后一天上课。　*The last day of school.*

Yíhuìr jiàn　一会儿见。　*See you soon.*

4.6　Saying how long you do something for

Now you can:

ask someone how long they spend or spent doing something:

Tā měi tiān liànxí duō cháng shíjiān?
他每天练习多长时间?

Tā shàngkè shàngle duō cháng shíjiān?
她上课上了多长时间?

say how long you spend doing something:

Wǒmen kèjiān xiūxi shí fēnzhōng.
我们课间休息十分钟。

Wǒmen zhōngwǔ xiūxi liǎng xiǎoshí líng shí fēnzhōng.
我们中午休息两小时零十分钟。
Tā xīngqīliù shàng wǔ gè xiǎoshí de kè.
她星期六上五个小时的课。

say how long you spent doing something:
Wǒ liànxíle yí gè xiǎoshí.　我练习了一个小时。
Wǒ pǎobù pǎole shíwǔ fēnzhōng.
　我跑步跑了十五分钟。
Wǒ qíle èrshí fēnzhōng de chē.　我骑了二十分钟的车。

Useful expressions
Nǐ zhēn shì gè dàmángrén!　你真是个大忙人!
　What a Busy Bee you are!
(LTR) Wǒ dōu zuòcuò le!　我都做错了!　*I've done it all
　wrong! I've got them all wrong!*

4.7　Talking about exams

Now you can:

say you are having an exam or test:
Wǒmen jīntiān kǎo wàiyǔ.　我们今天考外语。
Wǒmen míngtiān yǒu lìshǐ cèyàn.
　我们明天有历史测验。

talk about exam results:
Nǐ kǎo de zěnmeyàng?　你考得怎么样?
Wǒ kǎo de bù hǎo.　我考得不好。
Tā lìshǐ kǎo de fēicháng hǎo!　他历史考得非常好!
Wǒ shùxué déle 20 fēn.　我数学得了20分。
Wǒ kǎole/déle 62 fēn.　我考了/得了62分。
Wǒ jígé le.　我及格了。
Wǒ bù jígé.　我不及格。

Useful expressions
Bù zěnmeyàng. 不怎么样。 *Not very well. Not very
　good. Pretty badly.*
Méi shìr! 没事儿! *No problem!*
Néng jígé jiù xíng. 能及格就行。 *So long as I/you
　pass, that'll do.*
Zěnme la? 怎么啦? *What's the matter?*

学会写字 第十六课 (Xuéhuì xiě zì Dì-shíliù kè) (4.1)

● 汉字表

千	qiān *thousand*	
百	bǎi *hundred*	
会	huì *can; to know how to; meeting; party; be likely to*	
写	xiě *to write*	

对话

1. A: 我们学校有一千五百个学生，
   有六十九个老师。
   B: 你们学校人真多！
   A: 你们呢？
   B: 我们学校有四百个学生，十二个老师。
   A: 哦，你们学校真小。

2. A: 你学了多少个汉字？
   B: 我会写一百七十个汉字。

学会写字 第十七课

(Xuéhuì xiě zì
Dì-shíqī kè) (4.2)

● 汉字表

级	jí grade; level; rank	共	gòng share
班	bān class; (work) shift	节	jié (measure word)
时	shí time	候	hòu time; season

1. 对话
   A: 你上哪个中学？
   B: 四十九中。
   A: 有多少个学生？
   B: 一千二百多个学生。

2. 短文
   　　我叫谢汉生，今年上九年级。九年级一共有七个班。我在五班。
   　　我每天早上八点上学，九点上课。我们上午上四节课。下午，有时候上两节课，有时候上一节课。我们三点二十下课。下了课我常常去球场打球。我四点半回家。

学会写字 第十八课 (Xuéhuì xiě zì Dì-shíbā kè) (4.3)

● 汉字表

想	xiǎng *to think; want*	里	lǐ *in; inside*
以	yǐ *according to*	可	kě *can may; (used for emphasis)*
许	xǔ *allow; permit*		

对话

A: 晚上我想去同学家里玩儿，可以吗？

B: 几点回来？

A: 十一点。

B: 十一点？不行，太晚了。

A: 那我十点回来，行吗？

B: 好，不许太晚了！

A: 好。

学会写字 第十九课

(Xuéhuì xiě zì
Dì-shíjiǔ kè)   (4.4)

● 汉字表

英	yīng *(abbrev. of* 英国 *England)*	文	wén *writing;* *script;* *language*	数	shù *number*
难	nán *difficult*	练	liàn *practise;* *train*	习	xí *practise;* *review*
就	jiù *right away;* *right after;* *only; just;* *precisely*	听	tīng *hear; listen*	记	jì *remember*

短文 🎞

　　我叫许英。我明年上十一年级。我明年想上数学和中文。

　　很多人说，中文和数学很难学，我觉得 (juéde) 也对也不对。学数学要多做练习，练习做得多，就不觉得难了。学中文也要多听，多看，多记。听得多，看得多，记得多，就不觉得难了。

　　你说，我说得对不对？

学会写字 第二十课 (Xuéhuì xiě zì Dì-èrshí kè)

(4.5)

● 汉字表

第	dì *(indicating ordinal number)*	复	fù *again*	旧	jiù *old; used; worn*
新	xīn *new*	为	wèi *for*	帮	bāng *to help*

对话 ▣

A: 今天第一、二节课，
　　你怎么没来？

B: 我家里有事儿。
　　今天是复习旧课
　　还是上新课？

A: 上新课，作业还不少呢！

B: 是吗？昨天的作业我还没
　　做呢！

A: 你为什么没做？

B: 我家里有事儿。
　　没有时间复习。

A: 这样吧，我下午三点以后
　　没事儿，我可以帮你复习。

B: 太好了，谢谢你！

学会写字 第二十一课 (Xuéhuì xiě zì Dì-èrshíyī kè) (4.6)

● 汉字表

	gěi to give; to; for		cóng from		dào up to; up until; arrive; reach; go to; leave for
给		从		到	
吃	chī to eat	饭	fàn meal; cooked rice	钟	zhōng time measured in hours and minutes; clock

短文 📼

王老师是北京人。他在中国教 (jiāo) 了十年的汉语，现在在我们学校教我们汉语。

他每星期给我们上八个小时的汉语课。他教得很好，大家都喜欢他。

每天中午，从十二点半到一点半是我们吃午饭的时间。王老师常常和我们一起吃饭。这样同学们就可以练习说汉语，大家都很高兴。

王老师每天晚上看半个小时的电视，学一个小时的英语。睡觉以前还看二十分钟的英语小说。现在他的英语也说得很好。

王老师是个好老师。我们大家都喜欢他。

学会写字 第二十二课

● 汉字表

考	kǎo *give or take an examination*	试	shì *to try; test; examination*	题	tí *topic; subject; title; problem*
完	wán *finish; complete*	容	róng *to permit; allow*	易	yì *easy*

对话 📼

A: 今天的考试,你考得怎么样?

B: 还可以。
   我有一个题没有做完。

A: 是不是考得很难?

B: 不难,挺容易的,
   可是题太多了!

FOR AFTER CLASS ... 课外活动

● 小话剧 🔊 (Xiǎo huàjù)

"她是我妹妹"

人物： 李先生　　　　　50 岁左右
　　　 李先生的女儿　22 岁
　　　 小伙子　　　　　18 岁
　　　 乘客

Scene

On a bus at the bus terminus. All the seats are occupied except a seat for two passengers. Whistling a tune, the young man boards the bus. He looks around and sees the empty seat. He quickly strides towards it and sits down, taking up the whole seat. Moments later, Mr Li boards the bus carrying a briefcase in one hand and a newspaper in the other. He walks over to where the young man is sitting.

李先生： 小伙子,请你往里坐坐,好吗?

小伙子： 这儿有人坐!

李先生： 哦,对不起。

(moves to the end of the bus, puts his briefcase down, leans against a pole and reads the paper)

(A young woman boards the bus and moves down the aisle.)

小伙子： *(sees her)* 请坐,这个坐位没人!

女儿： 谢谢!

小伙子： 没什么!

(Mr Li rolls up his newspaper. He walks over and taps the young man on the shoulder)

李先生： 喂,你刚才不是说这儿有人坐吗?

女儿： *(looks up)* 哦!……

小伙子： *(before she can continue)* 没事儿! 你坐!

(hastily gets up, leads Mr Li away)

李先生： 你刚才不是说这儿有人坐吗?

(The young woman laughs to herself.)

小伙子： 是,是,我说的就是她,…… 她 …… 是我妹妹!

李先生： 哦? *(smiles)* 那太好了!

(hits the young man with the rolled-up newspaper)

你给我滚下去!

小伙子： 哎哟！
你，你干什么打
人？！

李先生： 滚下去！

小伙子： 哎哟！哎哟！不许
打人！

李先生： 你这样的儿子，
就得教训教训！

小伙子： 什么？！儿子？
老先生，您看错人了！

女儿： 爸，你别理他！

小伙子： 什么？！

(to young woman)

你是 ……。

李先生： 她是我女儿！

小伙子： 啊？

(rushes off the bus, as Mr Li sits down beside the young woman)

乘客： 哈，哈，哈！

Notes:

1. *Qǐng nǐ wàng lǐ zuòzuo* — *Wàng* is a preposition meaning 'to' or 'toward'.

2. *Nǐ gāngcái bú shì shuō zhèr yǒu rén zuò ma?* — *Bú shì...ma?* forms a rhetorical question and lends exphasis to the sentence — 'Didn't you say that this seat was occupied?'

3. *Nǐ gěi wǒ gǔn xiaqu!* — *Gěi wǒ* expresses the resolve on the part of the speaker and is often used for emphasis in commands. More examples:

    Nǐ gěi wǒ zuòxia!
    Gěi wǒ qù shuìjiào!

4. *Nǐ bié lǐ tā le!* — Note that *lǐ* 理 (pay attention to) is more often used in the negative. For example:

    Tā bù lǐ wǒ le.   She ignores me now.
    Tā bú ài (爱) *lǐ rén.*   He's stand-offish.

生词

话剧 huàjù *play, drama*
小伙子 xiǎo huǒzi *(colloquial) lad, young fellow*
乘客 chéngkè *passenger*
往 wàng *to, toward*
坐位 zuòwèi *seat; place to sit*

滚 gǔn *get out, get away, beat it*
滚下去 gǔn xiaqu *get off (the bus)*
儿子 érzi *son*
教训 jiàoxun *teach someone a lesson*
理 lǐ *pay attention to; acknowledge*
女儿 nǚ'ér *daughter*
啊 ǎ *(exclamation expressing surprise) oh?*

笑话 🔘

1 老师： 小华，同学们在学校里
最常用的三个字是什么？

小华：　不知道。

老师：　对了！

2　孩子：　今天考试，我一定考第一！

爸爸：　你怎么知道？

孩子：　补考的学生就我一个！

3　小明：　看，叔叔给了我一个礼物！

妈妈：　你有没有说谢谢？

小明：　没有。

妈妈：　要说谢谢。快去说。

小明：　不用说。

妈妈：　为什么？！

小明：　叔叔给你礼物的时候，你说谢谢，

　　　　他说"不用谢"！

4　我来说一个笑话。

妈妈问小明，"你今天数学考得怎么样？"
小明说，"我就错了一道题。"妈妈听了非常高兴，
她说，"啊，太好了！老师一共考了几道题？""十二道"，
小明说。妈妈更高兴了，"十二道题！那你答对了
十一道，真是好孩子！"小明说："不，那十一道题
我都不懂。"

Notes:

1. *Bǔkǎo de xuéshēng jiù wǒ yí gè* — Jiù (就) means 'only' and is stressed when uttered.
2. *Wǒ lái shuō yí gè xiàohuà* — Lái (来) indicates intention to do something.

生词

笑话　xiàohuà　*joke*
　说笑话　shuō xiàohuà　*tell a joke*
补考　bǔkǎo　*supplementary test*

叔叔　shūshu　*form of address for a man about one's father's age; uncle (father's younger brother)*
礼物　lǐwù　*present*
答　dá　*to answer*

Unit vocabulary

Vocabulary items for each unit area are listed in *pinyin* alphabetical order (see explanation on page 183).

Unit 1 你喜欢做什么?

1.1 Talking about your likes and dislikes

ài 爱 *to love, like . . .*
bú tài . . . 不太…… *not very . . .*
chángcháng 常常 *often*
chàng 唱 *to sing*
chàng gē 唱歌 *to sing*
Chén Huá 陈华 *(name)*
chūmén 出门 *to go out*
diànyǐng 电影 *film, movie*
diànzǐ 电子 *electron, electronic*
　　diànzǐ yóuxì 电子游戏 *video or computer game*
dōu 都 *all*
duànliàn (shēntǐ) 锻炼(身体) *to take physical exercise*
fēicháng 非常 *extremely*
gē 歌 *song*
huán(gěi) . . . 还(给)…… *return to . . .*
kě'ài 可爱 *lovable, likeable*
kěyǐ 可以 *can, may*
lánqiú 篮球 *basketball*
Lán Xīn 蓝新 *(name)*
Liú Xīnxīng 刘新星 *(name)*
mǎi 买 *to buy*
mǎi dōngxi 买东西 *to shop*
méi yìsi 没意思 *uninteresting; boring*
mén 门 *door, gate*
páiqiú 排球 *volleyball*
pǎo 跑 *to run*
pǎobù 跑步 *to run*
pīngpāngqiú 乒乓球 *pingpong, table tennis*
qī 期 *period of time*
Sàlì 萨莉 *Sally*
shēntǐ 身体 *body*
tī 踢 *to kick; play (football)*
　　tī zúqiú 踢足球 *play football*
tiāntiān 天天 *every day, daily*
tiào 跳 *to dance*
　　tiàowǔ 跳舞 *to dance*
Wáng Bīn 王彬 *(name)*
Wáng Bīng 王冰 *(name)*
wánr 玩儿 *to play, enjoy oneself*
wǔ 舞 *dance*
xǐhuan 喜欢 *to like*
ya 呀 *(sentence particle)*
yì jiā rén 一家人 *whole family*
yīnyuèmí 音乐迷 *music enthusiast*

yǒu yìsi 有意思 *interesting*
yóuxì 游戏 *game*
yùndòng 运动 *sport*
zázhì 杂志 *magazine*
Zěnme la? 怎么啦? *What's the matter? Why?*
zúqiú 足球 *football*
zuì 最 *most*
zuò 做 *to do*
　　zuò fàn 做饭 *do the cooking, prepare a meal*

Learn to read

Wáng Yàwén 王亚文 *(name)*

Learn to write　Lesson 1

Wáng Xīng 王星 *(name)*

1.2 Asking a '吗' question another way

búcuò 不错 *not bad; pretty good*
cuò 错 *wrong, mistake; (complement of result)*
Dānní 丹尼 *Danny*
hǎokàn 好看 *(of something seen or read) good*
jiù 就 *(ushers in a result); then*
lái 来 *come*
tīngshuō 听说 *to hear (about something)*
xiǎng 想 *intend, want to; think*
xíng 行 *be all right; OK*

1.3 Saying you've finished doing something

dài 带 *bring; take; carry*
gēn 跟 *with; and*
gēn . . . jiè 跟……借 *borrow from . . .*
Lín Huá 林华 *(name)*
ná 拿 *take*
náqu 拿去 *take away*
qiúpāi 球拍 *racket, bat*
Xiǎo Huá 小华 *(name)*
yòng 用 *to use*

Learn to read

Dàtóng 大同 *(name)*

1.4 Saying what you can do

àn 按 *to press*
Bú kèqi. 不客气。 *(polite response to thanks)*
chéngxù 程序 *programme; procedure*
dǎ 打 *to hit, strike*
děi 得 *must, have to*
huì 会 *can, know how to; be good at*
gàn 干 *to do*
jiàn 键 *key (of a keyboard)*
jiǎng 讲 *explain*
jiāo 教 *teach, instruct*
kāishǐ 开始 *begin*
kěshì 可是 *but, however*
Líndá 琳达 *Linda*
Liú Xīn 刘新 *(name)*
máng 忙 *busy*
néng 能 *can, be able to*
qiú 求 *to beg, request*
shì 试 *to try; to test*
wǎngqiú 网球 *tennis*
xiān 先 *first; before; earlier*
zìmǔ 字母 *(alphabet) letter*

Learn to write   Lesson 4

zhème... 这么…… *so...*

1.5 Describing actions

chīfàn 吃饭 *to eat; to have a meal*
dǎzì 打字 *to type*
de 得 *(structural particle)*
Dīng 丁 *(family name)*
  Dīng Lì 丁力 *(name)*
duō 多 *much, a lot*
fàn 饭 *food; cooked rice*
gāoxìng 高兴 *happy*
gèng 更 *even more, still more*
gǔdiǎn 古典 *classical*
  gǔdiǎn yīnyuè 古典音乐 *classical music*
hǎotīng 好听 *melodious, pleasant to listen to*
huì 会 *know how to; be good at*
juéde 觉得 *to think, feel*
kànlai 看来 *it seems; it looks as if*
Lánlán 兰兰 *(name)*
liǎ 俩 *two*
liúlì 流利 *fluent*
luàn 乱 *in disorder, in a confusion; disorder, chaos*
Mǎ 马 *(family name)*
  Mǎ Xiǎoqīng 马小青 *(name)*
Méi shénme. 没什么。 *It's nothing.*
míngbai 明白 *to understand*
nǎli 哪里 *(polite response to praise)*
qiúmí 球迷 *ball game enthusiast*
rúcǐ 如此 *like that*
tǐyù yùndòng 体育运动 *sport*
xiě zì 写字 *to write*
yóu 游 *to swim*
yuánlái rúcǐ 原来如此 *So that's how it is...*

Yuēhàn 约汉 *John*
zěnyàng 怎样 *how*
zì 字 *character; word*
zìjǐ 自己 *self*
Zhōngguóhuà 中国话 *Chinese (language)*

Learn to read

shìde 是的 *yes; right; that's it*
tǐyù zhī jiā 体育之家 *family of sports enthusiasts*
zhī 之 *of (classical)*

1.6 Telephoning your friends

bómǔ 伯母 *aunt (form of address); father's elder brother's wife*
dǎ diànhuà 打电话 *to telephone*
  dǎcuò 打错 *ring a wrong number*
diànhuà 电话 *telephone*
  diànhuàbù 电话簿 *telephone directory*
diànhuà hàomǎ 电话号码 *telephone number*
gāngcái 刚才 *just now*
gěi 给 *to give; to, for*
  gěi...dǎ diànhuà 给……打电话 *telephone (someone)*
  gěi...huí diànhuà 给……回电话 *make a return call to...*
hàomǎ 号码 *number*
huí 回 *return*
  huí diànhuà 回电话 *a return phone call; to return a phone call*
  huílai 回来 *come back, return*
jiālǐ 家里 *home; the family*
jiē 接 *receive*
  jiē diànhuà 接电话 *take a phone call*
jiù 就 *at once, right away*
ràng 让 *let, allow; get someone to (do something)*
yāo 幺 *one*
yàng 样 *appearance; shape; kind; type*
zài 在 *at, in, on*
  zàijiā 在家 *be at home*
zhèiyàng 这样 *like this; this way; so; such*

Learn to read

Wáng Xiǎomíng 王小明 *(name)*

Learn to write   Lesson 6

jiào 叫 *ask, tell (someone to do something)*

Unit 2 我穿什么好?

2.1 What are they wearing?

bù shǎo 不少 *quite a lot*
chángkù 长裤 *long pants, trousers*
chènshān 衬衫 *shirt*

chūqu   出去   *go out*
chuān   穿   *wear; (of clothes) put on*
chuānshàng   穿上   *(of clothes) put on*
dài   戴   *(of headgear, glasses, badge) wear*
dǐng   顶   *(MW for hat)*
Dōngdōng   冬冬   *(name)*
duǎnkù   短裤   *shorts*
fù   副   *(MW for spectcles)*
gòu   够   *enough*
hǎibiānr   海边儿   *seaside*
hànshān   汗衫   *T-shirt*
jiàn   件   *(MW for clothes)*
kuài   块   *(MW for watch)*
lǐngdài   领带   *necktie*
máoyī   毛衣   *jumper*
màozi   帽子   *hat, cap*
mòjìng   墨镜   *sunglasses, dark glasses*
niúzǎikù   牛仔裤   *jeans*
píxié   皮鞋   *leather shoes*
qiúxié   球鞋   *gym shoes, sneakers*
qúnzi   裙子   *skirt*
shǎo   少   *less, few*
shuāng   双   *(MW); pair*
tào   套   *(MW); set*
tiáo   条   *(MW for clothes)*
wàzi   袜子   *socks*
wàitào   外套   *coat, jacket*
xīzhuāng   西装   *suit*
Xiǎo Yún   小云   *(name)*
xié   鞋   *shoes*
yào   要   *should, must, ought*
yīfu   衣服   *clothes, clothing*
yīnggāi   应该   *should, ought*
yùndòngfú   运动服   *tracksuit*

Learn to write   Lesson 7

dàyī   大衣   *overcoat*

2.2   How does it look?

cháng   长   *long*
    cháng yìdiǎnr de   长一点儿的   *longer one(s)*
dōngxi   东西   *thing*
duǎn   短   *short*
féi   肥   *(of clothes) loose, big*
fúwùyuán   服务员   *attendant; sales assistant*
fùzá   复杂   *complicated; (of style) fussy*
guài   怪   *weird, strange*
Hǎilún   海伦   *Helen*
hǎo jiǔ   好久   *for a long time*
    Hǎo jiǔ bú jiàn le!   好久不见了!   *Haven't seen you for a long time!*
héshēn   合身   *(of clothes) fit*
héshì   合适   *suitable, appropriate*
huā   花   *flower; (of style) flowery; gaudy*
jiàn   见   *see; (resultative complement)*
jǐn   紧   *tight*
jiǔ   久   *for a long time*

kùzi   裤子   *trousers, pants, slacks*
mǎi   买   *to buy*
    mǎi dōngxi   买东西   *to shop*
nánkàn   难看   *ugly, unattractive*
shímáo   时髦   *fashionable*
shūfu   舒服   *comfortable*
shuìyī   睡衣   *pyjamas*
suíbiàn   随便   *casual; random*
Wáng Yǒng   王勇   *(name)*
xīn   新   *new*
    xīncháo   新潮   *trendy; latest fashion*
yánsè   颜色   *colour*
yàngzi   样子   *style; appearance*
yìbān   一般   *common, ordinary*

Learn to read

hào   号   *size*

Learn to write   Lesson 8

shàngyī   上衣   *top (clothing)*

2.3   What colour is it?

bái(sè)   白(色)   *white*
cānjiā   参加   *attend, take part in*
chéng(sè)   橙(色)   *orange*
chuān qilai   穿起来   *put on, wear*
gēn…pèi   跟……配   *go with…; match…*
hēi(sè)   黑(色)   *black*
hóng(sè)   红(色)   *red*
huáng(sè)   黄(色)   *yellow*
huī(sè)   灰(色)   *grey*
huì   会   *party; meeting; gathering*
lán(sè)   蓝(色)   *blue*
lǜ(sè)   绿(色)   *green*
pèi   配   *match*
qilai   起来   *(complement indicating an action beginning and continuing)*
qiǎn   浅   *light, pale*
    qiǎn lánsè   浅蓝色   *light blue*
shēn   深   *deep*
    shēn lánsè   深蓝色   *deep blue*
shēngrìhuì   生日会   *birthday party*
Tuōní   托尼   *Tony, Toni*
zǐ(sè)   紫(色)   *purple*
zōng(sè)   棕(色)   *brown*

Learn to read

pèishàng   配上   *to match; match up*
qǐng   请   *to invite*
yì shēn(r)   一身(儿)   *outfit (of clothes)*

Learn to write   Lesson 9

xiàofú   校服   *school uniform*

2.4   Describing people

bízi　鼻子　*nose*
bózi　脖子　*neck*
Chén　陈　*(family name)*
dùzi　肚子　*belly, abdomen*
ěrduo　耳朵　*ear*
gēbo　胳膊　*arm*
gèzi　个子　*height, build*
guāngtóu　光头　*bald*
háizi　孩子　*child*
húzi　胡子　*beard, moustache*
jiǎo　脚　*foot*
jiànmiàn　见面　*to meet (someone)*
jīnsè　金色　*golden*
juǎn　卷　*curly*
liǎn　脸　*face*
Lín Qīng　林青　*(name)*
máo　毛　*hair; fur*
nán de　男的　*male; male person*
nǚ de　女的　*female; female person*
nǚ háizi　女孩子　*girl*
pífū　皮肤　*skin*
pūtōng　扑通　*Plop! Splash!*
qíguài　奇怪　*strange, weird*
qīngwā　青蛙　*frog*
shǒu　手　*hand*
shuǐ　水　*water*
tiào　跳　*to jump*
　tiàoxia shuǐ　跳下水　*jump into the water*
tóu　头　*head*
tóufa　头发　*hair*
tuǐ　腿　*leg*
wěiba　尾巴　*tail*
yǎnjìng　眼镜　*glasses*
yǎnjing　眼睛　*eye*
yàngr　样儿　*appearance, shape*
yuán　圆　*round*
zhǎng　长　*grow; develop*
zhí　直　*straight*
zuǐba　嘴巴　*mouth*

Learn to read

nǚpéngyou　女朋友　*girlfriend*
xiǎoháir　小孩儿　*child*
shīzi　狮子　*lion*
　shīzigǒu　狮子狗　*Shitzu (breed of dog)*

Learn to write   Lesson 10

nán háir　男孩儿　*boy*

Unit 3　我的书在哪儿了？

3.1   Indicating where someone or something is

bàn　办　*do; manage; attend to*
　bàngōng　办公　*handle official business*
　bàngōnglóu　办公楼　*office building*
　bàngōngshì　办公室　*office*
céng　层　*storey; floor; layer, (MW)*
duìmiàn　对面　*opposite*
èr lóu　二楼　*first floor*
fángzi　房子　*house*
gébì　隔壁　*next door (of room, house, etc.)*
hǎoxiàng　好象　*seem, appear*
hòumian　后面　*behind*
jiàoshìlóu　教室楼　*classroom building*
jiù　就　*exactly, precisely*
lǐmiàn　里面　*inside*
lóu　楼　*storeyed building; storey, floor*
　lóushàng　楼上　*upstairs*
　lóuxià　楼下　*downstairs*
pángbiān(r)　旁边（儿）　*beside*
Píngping　萍萍　*(name)*
qiánmian　前面　*in front*
shàngmian　上面　*on, above*
tóu(r)　头儿　*top, end*
wàimian　外面　*outside*
xiàmian　下面　*under, below*
yòubian(r)　右边（儿）　*on the right; right side*
zhōngjiān　中间　*centre, middle*
zuǒbian(r)　左边（儿）　*on the left; left side*

Learn to read

huí　回　*(MW for number of times)*
yī céng　一层　*ground floor*

3.2   What are they doing there?

cāibùzháo　猜不着　*give up (be unable to guess)*
chēzhàn　车站　*bus stop, train station*
děng　等　*wait*
　děng rén　等人　*wait for someone*
gōngkè　功课　*schoolwork; homework*
hāi　咳　*(exclamation indicating sadness or surprise)*
fùxí　复习　*revise; revision*
　fùxí gōngkè　复习功课　*revise school work*
jiànshēncāo　健身操　*fitness exercises; aerobics*
jiào　叫　*to call (someone)*
jiē diànhuà　接电话　*answer the telephone*
nàr　那儿　*there*
　nǐ nàr　你那儿　*there (where you are); your place*

qiúchǎng   球场   *tennis court, football field etc.*
rén   人   *person; somebody*
shàng   上   *on*
tǎorénxián   讨人嫌   *annoy someone/people*
túshūguǎn   图书馆   *library*
wǒmen zhèr   我们这儿   *here (where we are); our place*
zhèr   这儿   *here*

Learn to read

jiù   就   *only; merely; just*

Learn to write Lesson 12

gēn . . . shuōhuà   跟……说话   *speak with . . .*
kànjiàn   看见   *see*
shuōhuà   说话   *speak, talk, say*

3.3   Talking about your school

bān   班   *class; (work) shift*
cāochǎng   操场   *sports ground (in a school)*
cèsuǒ   厕所   *lavatory, toilet*
Chén Xīn   陈新   *(name)*
chū'èr   初二   *2nd year of junior high school*
chūyī   初一   *1st year of junior high school*
dǎkāi   打开   *to open*
dàmén   大门   *main entrance*
dài   带   *take, bring (someone somewhere)*
éi   诶   *(exclamation expressing surprise, astonishment)*
fùjìn   附近   *nearby*
huānyíng   欢迎   *welcome*
jì   记   *to remember*
    jì qilai   记起来   *remember*
jiāo   交   *hand in; deliver*
    jiāogěi . . .   交给……   *hand in to . . .; deliver to . . .*
Lǐ   李   *(family name)*
    Lǐ Fāng   李方   *(name)*
lǐtáng   礼堂   *hall, auditorium*
ménkǒu   门口   *entrance, doorway*
nán cèsuǒ   男厕所   *male toilet*
niánjí   年级   *year, grade, form*
nǚ cèsuǒ   女厕所   *female toilet*
rènshi   认识   *know (someone)*
wàng   忘   *forget*
xīnshēng   新生   *new student*
xiǎomàibù   小卖部   *tuckshop*
yī lóu   一楼   *ground floor*
zì   字   *writing*

Learn to read

lóufáng   楼房   *storeyed building*
zuì yòubian   最右边   *far right*

3.4   Indicating a change

cí   词   *word*
huà   话   *word; talk*
jì bù qilai   记不起来   *cannot remember*
jù   句   *(MW for sentence) line*

wǒ zhèr   我这儿   *here (where I am)*
yìsi   意思   *meaning*

Learn to read

jiànwàng   健忘   *forgetful*
Lín Hóng   林红   *(name)*
Xiǎo Hóng   小红   *(name)*

Learn to write   Lesson 14

lán   蓝   *(family name); blue*
Lán Lán   蓝蓝   *(name)*

3.5   Giving someone your address

Ān   安   *Ann*
bāng . . . de máng   帮……的忙   *help (someone)*
bāngmáng   帮忙   *to help*
dào   到   *arrive*
dìzhǐ   地址   *address*
dōng   东   *east*
    dōngnán   东南   *southeast*
gànmá   干吗   *why, what for*
guì   贵   *(polite expression) your*
    Nín guì xìng?   您贵姓?   *May I ask your name?*
huāyuán   花园   *garden*
jìnlai   进来   *come in*
nán   南   *south*
qū   区   *region, district*

Learn to read

Dōngsì   东四   *(place name)*
hǎo zhǎo   好找   *easy to find*
Sāntiáo   三条   *(place name)*

Unit 4   你喜欢上什么课?

4.1   Counting from 100 to 9999

dào   到   *to, up to*
bǎi   百   *hundred*
qiān   千   *thousand*

4.2   Talking about school life

bān   班   *class*
    bānzhǔrèn   班主任   *teacher in charge of class*
bú dào   不到   *less than*
chà bù duō   差不多   *about*
chūzhōng   初中   *junior high school*
Dīng Lìměi   丁丽美   *(name)*
dōu   都   *both*
duō   多   *(with numeral) over, more than*
hé   和   *and; with*
    hé . . . tóngbān   和……同班   *be in the same class as . . .*

jǐ 几 (after numeral) more than
jié 节 (MW for lesson)
Lǐ Qiáng 李强 (name)
Lín Yīng 林英 (name)
nánshēng 男生 male student
nǚshēng 女生 female student
tóngbān 同班 same class; be in the same class
yígòng 一共 altogether, in all

Learn to read

Nán Sì Zhōng 男四中 (abbrev.) No. 4 Boys High
    School
xiàozhǎng 校长 school principal
yì tiān 一天 a day

Learn to write   Lesson 17

Xiè Hànshēng 谢汉生 (name)

4.3 Asking permission and telling people what or what not to do

bùxíng 不行 won't do
bùxǔ 不许 must not; not allowed to
búyào 不要 must not, don't
chǎo 吵 noisy, to make a noise, to disturb
chī dōngxi 吃东西 eat (something)
chídào 迟到 be late
chuāng 窗 window
dào 道 (MW for exam, test question tí 题)
…de shíhou ……的时候 when…; during…
gāi 该 ought to, should
hā 哈 ha (onomatopoeia for laughter)
kāihuì 开会 hold or attend a meeting
kān 看 to look after, take care of
    kān háizi 看孩子 look after children; babysit
Liú 刘 (family name)
qiānbǐ 铅笔 pencil
shēng 声 sound; voice
tí 题 examination questions; problem; topic
tíng 停 to stop
    tíngchē 停车 to park
wèi shénme 为什么 why
wù 勿 (indicates prohibition)
xīyān 吸烟 to smoke
xiǎo shēng 小声 (of sound) softly
xiào 笑 to laugh, smile
yán'gé 严格 strict
yǐhòu 以后 after
yǐqián 以前 before
yùxí 预习 prepare lessons before class
zài 再 again; once more

4.4 Talking about school subjects

āiyō 哎哟 (exclamation expressing surprise, pain)
bié 别 don't
dìlǐ 地理 Geography
hǎo 好 be easy (to do); (complement of result indicating completion)
huàxué 化学 Chemistry

jiù 旧 old, worn
kēxué 科学 Science
kè 课 lesson, class; school subject
lìshǐ 历史 History
měishù 美术 Art
mén 门 (measure word for school subjects)
nán xué 难学 difficult to study
shēngwù 生物 Biology
shùxué 数学 Mathematics
tǎoyàn 讨厌 disagreeable; to dislike
tǐyù 体育 Physical Education
wàiyǔ 外语 foreign languages
wán 完 finish; (complement of result)
wùlǐ 物理 Physics
xiǎnghǎo 想好 to consider and come to a conclusion
yìqǐ 一起 together; in company
yǒu yòng 有用 useful
yǔwén 语文 language and literature; Chinese (subject)
zuòwán 做完 to finish, complete

Learn to write   Lesson 19

Xǔ 许 (family name)
    Xǔ Yīng 许英 (name)

4.5 Talking about your timetable

cái 才 then (and only then)
cóng 从 from
dì 第 (prefix indicating an ordinal number)
fàngxīn 放心 feel relieved; set one's mind at rest
huódòng 活动 activity, to have an activity
jièyòng 借用 borrow
kèchéngbiǎo 课程表 school timetable
kèjiāncāo 课间操 physical exercises during break
kèwài 课外 extra-curricular
    kèwài huódòng 课外活动 extra-curricular activity
xià yì jié (kè) 下一节(课) next class
xiàohuì 校会 school assembly
yídìng 一定 certainly, definitely
zǎo 早 early
zìxí 自习 self-study session; study on one's own
zhèngzhì 政治 politics

Learn to read

xīngqītiān 星期天 Sunday
zuìhòu 最后 last; final

4.6 Saying how long you do something for

dàmángrén 大忙人 very busy person
duō cháng 多长 how long
fēnzhōng 分钟 minute
lèisǐ 累死 extremely tired
liànxí 练习 practise
shíjiān 时间 time

...sǐ　……死　*(indicating an extreme) extremely*
wǎngqiúchǎng　网球场　*tennis court*
xiǎoshí　小时　*hour*
xiǎozǔ　小组　*small group; group*
xiūxi　休息　*to rest*

Learn to read

hé...yìqǐ　和……一起　*together with...*
Huáng　黄　*(family name)*
jiàndào　见到　*see*
zuòcuò　做错　*do wrongly*

Learn to write　Lesson 21

gěi...shàngkè　给……上课　*give...a lesson*

4.7　Talking about exams

bù zěnmeyàng　不怎么样　*not very good*
cèyàn　测验　*test*
dé　得　*get, obtain*
fēn　分　*mark*
huábīng　滑冰　*to skate, skating*
jí　极　*extreme*
　...jí le　……极了　*extremely...*
jígé　及格　*to pass (an exam); be up to the standard*
jǐnzhāng　紧张　*be tense, anxious*
kǎo　考　*to give or take an exam*
　kǎoshì　考试　*exam*
kùn　困　*sleepy*

Learn to read

huì　会　*be sure (likely) to*

Vocabulary

1. Single-character entries are listed in *pinyin* alphabetical order. Those with the same spelling but different tone are arranged according to tone. Those with both the same spelling and tone are arranged according to number of strokes. Those with the same number of strokes are listed by stroke type in the following order: 丶,一,丨,丿,一, beginning with the first stroke.

2. The above-mentioned rules also apply to compounds appearing under single-character entries beginning with the second character of the compound.

3. Likewise, the same rules apply to isolated compounds (i.e. compounds not listed under single-character entries) starting with the first character.

A

Ālún 阿伦 Alan
a 啊 (particle indicating an exclamation or affirmation)
āiyō 哎哟 (exclamation expressing surprise, pain)
ǎi 矮 (of height) short
ài 爱 to love, like
Ān 安 Ann
Ānnà 安娜 Anna
àn 按 to press

B

bā 八 eight
bàba 爸爸 father
ba 吧 (modal particle)
... ba? ......吧? (asking for confirmation)
bái(sè) 白(色) white
    Bái Yún 白云 (name)
bǎi 百 hundred
bān 班 class; (work) shift
    bānzhǔrèn 班主任 teacher in charge of class
bàn 办 do; manage; attend to
    bàngōng 办公 handle official business
    bàngōnglóu 办公楼 office building
    bàngōngshì 办公室 office
bàn 半 half
bāng 帮 to help
    bāng ... de máng 帮......的忙 help (someone)
    bāngmáng 帮忙 to help
Bǎoluó 保罗 Paul
Běijīng 北京 Beijing (Peking)
běn 本 (MW for book, novel)
bízi 鼻子 nose
bǐ 笔 writing instrument
Bǐdé 彼得 Peter
biǎo 表 table; list; watch
bié 别 don't
bómǔ 伯母 aunt (form of address; father's elder brother's wife)
bózi 脖子 neck
bù 不 not
búcuò 不错 not bad; pretty good

bú dào 不到 less than
Bú kèqi. 不客气 (polite response to thanks)
bù shǎo 不少 quite a lot
bú tài ... 不太...... not very ...
bùxíng 不行 won't do
bùxǔ 不许 must not; not allowed to
búyào 不要 must not, don't
búyòng 不用 need not
    Búyòng xiè. 不用谢 (polite response) Don't mention it.
bù zěnmeyàng 不怎么样 not very good

C

cāi 猜 guess
    cāibùzháo 猜不着 give up (be unable to guess)
cái 才 then (and only then)
cānjiā 参加 attend, take part in
cāo 操 drill; set physical exercise
    cāochǎng 操场 sports ground (in a school)
cèsuǒ 厕所 lavatory, toilet
cèyàn 测验 test
céng 层 storey; floor; layer, (MW)
chà bù duō 差不多 about
cháng 长 long
    chángkù 长裤 long pants, trousers
    cháng yìdiǎnr de 长一点儿的 longer one(s)
chángcháng 常常 often
chàng 唱 to sing
    chàng gē 唱歌 to sing
chǎo 吵 noisy, to make a noise, to disturb
chē 车 vehicle
    chēzhàn 车站 bus stop, train station
Chén 陈 (family name)
    Chén Huá 陈华 (name)
    Chén Xīn 陈新 (name)
chènshān 衬衫 shirt
chéng(sè) 橙(色) orange
chéngxù 程序 programme; procedure
chī 吃 to eat
    chī dōngxi 吃东西 eat (something)
    chīfàn 吃饭 to have a meal

chídào 迟到 *be late*
chū'èr 初二 *2nd year of junior high school*
chūmén 出门 *to go out*
chūqu 出去 *go out*
chūyī 初一 *1st year of junior high school*
chūzhōng 初中 *junior high school*
chuān 穿 *wear; (of clothes) put on*
  chuān qilai 穿起来 *put on, wear*
  chūanshàng 穿上 *(of clothes) put on*
chuāng 窗 *window*
chuáng 床 *bed*
cí 词 *word*
cóng 从 *from*
cuò 错 *wrong, mistake; (complement of result)*

D

dǎ 打 *to hit, strike; to play (sport)*
  dǎ diànhuà 打电话 *to telephone*
  dǎcuò 打错 *ring a wrong number*
  dǎjià 打架 *to fight*
  dǎkāi 打开 *to open*
  dǎ qiú 打球 *to play ball games (except football)*
  dǎzì 打字 *to type*
dà 大 *big*
  dàjiā 大家 *everyone*
  dàmángrén 大忙人 *very busy person*
  dàmén 大门 *main entrance*
  dàxué 大学 *university*
  dàxuéshēng 大学生 *university student*
  dàyī 大衣 *coat; overcoat*
Dàtóng 大同 *(name)*
Dàwèi 大卫 *David*
dài 带 *bring, take, carry; take, bring someone (somewhere)*
dài 戴 *(of headgear, glasses, badge) wear*
Dānní 丹尼 *Danny*
dānyuán 单元 *unit*
dào 到 *arrive; to, up to*
dào 道 *(MW for exam, test question tí 题)*
dé 得 *get, obtain*
de 的 *(particle indicating the possessive and attributive)*
  …de shíhou ……的时候 *when…; during…*
de 得 *(structural particle)*
děi 得 *must, have to*
děng 等 *to wait*
  děng rén 等人 *wait for someone*
dì 第 *(prefix indicating an ordinal number, e.g. 第一 first, 第二 second)*
dìdi 弟弟 *younger brother*
dìlǐ 地理 *geography*
dìtú 地图 *map*
dìzhǐ 地址 *address*
diǎn 点 *o'clock*
diànchē 电车 *tram; trolley bus*
diànhuà 电话 *telephone*
  diànhuàbù 电话簿 *telephone directory*
  diànhuà hàomǎ 电话号码 *telephone number*
diànshì 电视 *television*
diànyǐng 电影 *film, movie*
diànzǐ 电子 *electron, electronic*

diànzǐ yóuxì 电子游戏 *video or computer game*
dǐng 顶 *(MW for hat)*
Dīng 丁 *(family name)*
  Dīng Lì 丁力 *(name)*
  Dīng Lìměi 丁丽美 *(name)*
diū 丢 *to lose*
  diū le 丢了 *be lost*
dōng 东 *east*
  dōngnán 东南 *southeast*
  Dōngsì 东四 *(place name)*
  dōngxi 东西 *thing*
Dōngdōng 冬冬 *(name)*
dǒng 懂 *to understand*
dòng 动 *move*
  dòngwù 动物 *animal*
dōu 都 *all; both*
dùzi 肚子 *belly, abdomen*
duǎn 短 *short*
  duǎnkù 短裤 *shorts*
duànliàn (shēntǐ) 锻炼(身体) *to take physical exercise*
duì 对 *correct; right; towards*
  duìbuqǐ 对不起 *sorry (apology)*
  duìmiàn 对面 *opposite*
duō 多 *many; much, a lot; (with numeral) over, more than*
  duō cháng 多长 *how long*
  duō dà 多大 *how big; how old (of age)*
  duōshao 多少 *how many*

E

è 饿 *be hungry*
éi 诶 *(exclamation expressing surprise, astonishment)*
ěrduo 耳朵 *ear*
èr 二 *two*
  èr lóu 二楼 *first floor*

F

fàn 饭 *food; cooked rice*
fángjiān 房间 *room*
fángzi 房子 *house*
fàngxīn 放心 *feel relieved; set one's mind at rest*
fàngxué 放学 *to finish school for the day*
fēicháng 非常 *extremely*
Fēifēi 非非 *(name)*
féi 肥 *(of animals) fat; (of clothes) loose, big*
fēn 分 *minute; mark*
  fēnzhōng 分钟 *minute*
fēng 风 *wind*
fúwùyuán 服务员 *attendant; sales assistant*
fù 副 *(MW for spectacles)*
fùjìn 附近 *nearby*
fùxí 复习 *revise, revision*
  fùxí gōngkè 复习功课 *revise school work*
fùzá 复杂 *complicated; (of style) fussy*

G

gāi 该 *ought to, should*
  Gāi nǐ le. 该你了。 *It's your turn.*
gǎn 赶 *to catch up with; to rush ... through*
  gǎn zuòyè 赶作业 *to catch up with homework*
gàn 干 *to do*
  gànmá 干吗 *why, what for*
gāngcái 刚才 *just now*
gāo 高 *high; tall*
  gāoxìng 高兴 *happy*
gē 歌 *song*
gēbo 胳膊 *arm*
gēge 哥哥 *elder brother*
gébì 隔壁 *next door (of room, house, etc.)*
gè 个 *(measure word)*
  gèzi 个子 *height, build*
gěi 给 *to give; to, for*
  gěi ... dǎ diànhuà 给……打电话 *telephone (someone)*
  gěi ... huí diànhuà 给……回电话 *make a return call to ...*
  gěi ... shàngkè 给……上课 *give ... a lesson*
gēn 跟 *with; and*
  gēn ... jiè 跟……借 *borrow from ...*
  gēn ... pèi 跟……配 *go with ...; match ...*
  gēn ... shuōhuà 跟……说话 *speak with ...*
gèng 更 *even more, more*
gōnggòng qìchē 公共汽车 *bus*
gōngkè 功课 *schoolwork; homework*
gǒu 狗 *dog*
gòu 够 *enough*
gǔdiǎn 古典 *classical*
  gǔdiǎn yīnyuè 古典音乐 *classical music*
guā 刮 *(of wind) to blow*
  guā fēng 刮风 *to be windy*
guài 怪 *weird, strange*
guāngtóu 光头 *bald*
guì 贵 *(polite) your*
  (Nín) guì xìng? (您)贵姓？ *May I ask your name?*
guó 国 *country, nation*

H

hā 哈 *ha (onomatopoeia for laughter)*
hāi 咳 *(exclamation indicating sadness or surprise)*
hái 还 *still, even; also, too, in addition, as well*
  hái kěyǐ 还可以 *all right; so so*
  háishi 还是 *or*
  háiyǒu 还有 *also; furthermore*
háizi 孩子 *child*
hǎibiānr 海边儿 *seaside*
Hǎilún 海伦 *Helen*
hànshān 汗衫 *T-shirt*
Hànyǔ 汉语 *Chinese language*
  Hànyǔ lǎoshī 汉语老师 *Chinese language teacher*
  Hànzì 汉字 *Chinese character*
    Hànzì biǎo 汉字表 *character list*
hǎo 好 *good; well; (complement of result indicating completion); be easy (to do)*
  Hǎo. 好 *All right. (agreeing to something)*
  Hǎo jiǔ bú jiàn le! 好久不见了！ *Haven't seen you for a long time!*

hǎokàn 好看 *good looking, attractive; (of something seen or read) good*
..., hǎo ma! ……好吗？ *Shall we ...? How about ...?*
hǎotīng 好听 *melodious, pleasant to listen to*
hǎowánr 好玩儿 *fun; amusing*
hǎoxiàng 好象 *seem, appear*
hǎo zhǎo 好找 *easy to find*
hào 号 *date; number; size*
  hàomǎ 号码 *number*
hé 和 *and; with*
  hé ... tóngbān 和……同班 *be in the same class as ...*
  hé ... yìqǐ 和……一起 *together with ...*
héshēn 合身 *(of clothes) fit*
héshì 合适 *suitable, appropriate*
hēi(sè) 黑色 *black*
hěn 很 *very*
hóng(sè) 红(色) *red*
hòumian 后面 *behind*
hòutiān 后天 *day after tomorrow*
húzi 胡子 *beard, moustache*
huā 花 *flower; (of style) flowery; gaudy*
  huāyuán 花园 *garden*
huábīng 滑冰 *to skate, ice skating*
huà 话 *word, talk*
huà 画 *to draw; to paint*
  huà(r) 画(儿) *picture*
huàxué 化学 *Chemistry*
huānyíng 欢迎 *welcome*
huán(gěi)…… 还(给)… *return to ...*
huáng 黄 *yellow; (surname)*
  huáng(sè) 黄(色) *yellow*
huī(sè) 灰(色) *grey*
huí 回 *return*
  huí diànhuà 回电话 *to return a telephone call*
  huí jiā 回家 *to return home*
  huílai 回来 *come back, return*
huì 会 *can, know how to; be good at; party; meeting; be sure (likely) to*
huódòng 活动 *activity, to have an activity*
huǒchē 火车 *train*

J

jí 极 *extreme*
  ... jí le ……极了 *extremely ...*
jígé 及格 *to pass (an exam); be up to the standard*
jǐ 几 *(after numeral) more than*
jì 记 *to remember*
  jì bù qilai 记不起来 *cannot remember*
  jì qilai 记起来 *remember*
jiā 加 *to add*
jiā 家 *family; home*
  jiālǐ 家里 *home; the family*
jiǎn 减 *to subtract*
jiàn 见 *see; (resultative complement)*
  ... jiàn! ……见！ *See you ...!*
  jiàndào 见到 *see*
jiàn 件 *(MW for clothes)*
jiàn 键 *key (of a keyboard)*
Jiànhuá 建华 *(name)*

jiànmiàn 见面 *to meet (someone)*
jiànshēncāo 健身操 *fitness exercises; aerobics*
jiànwàng 健忘 *forgetful*
jiǎng 讲 *explain*
jiāo 交 *hand in; deliver*
  jiāogěi... 交给······ *hand in to ...; deliver to...*
jiāo 教 *teach, instruct*
jiǎo 脚 *foot*
jiào 叫 *to be called; to call (someone); ask, tell (someone to do something)*
jiàoshì 教室 *classroom*
  jiàoshìlóu 教室楼 *classroom building*
jiē 接 *receive*
  jiē diànhuà 接电话 *take a phone call*
jié 节 *(MW for lesson)*
jiějie 姐姐 *elder sister*
jiè 借 *to borrow; to lend*
  jiè(gěi) 借(给) *lend to (someone)*
  jièyòng 借用 *borrow*
jièshào 介绍 *to introduce*
jīn 金 *gold*
  jīnsè 金色 *golden*
  jīnyú 金鱼 *gold fish*
jīnnián 今年 *this year*
jīntiān 今天 *today*
jǐn 紧 *tight*
  jǐnzhāng 紧张 *be tense, anxious*
jìn 进 *to enter*
  jìnlai 进来 *come in*
jiǔ 九 *nine*
jiǔ 久 *for a long time*
jiù 旧 *old, worn*
jiù 就 *(ushers in a result); then; at once, right away; exactly, precisely; only; merely; just*
jù 句 *(MW for sentence) line*
juǎn 卷 *curly*
juéde 觉得 *to think, feel*

K

kāihuì 开会 *hold or attend a meeting*
kāishǐ 开始 *begin*
kān 看 *to look after, take care of*
  kān háizi 看孩子 *look after children; babysit*
kàn 看 *to see; to look; to read; to watch*
  kàn diànshì 看电视 *to watch television*
  kànjiàn 看见 *see*
  kànkan 看看 *have a look*
  kànlai 看来 *it seems; it looks as if*
  kàn shū 看书 *to read (a book)*
kǎo 考 *to give or take an exam*
  kǎoshì 考试 *exam*
kēxué 科学 *Science*
kě...le 可······了 *extremely; very...*
kě'ài 可爱 *lovable, likeable*
kěshì 可是 *but, however*
kěyǐ 可以 *can, may*
kè 刻 *quarter (of an hour)*
kè 课 *lesson, class; school subject*
  kèběn 课本 *textbook*

kèchéngbiǎo 课程表 *school timetable*
kèjiān 课间 *break between classes at school*
  kèjiāncāo 课间操 *physical exercises during break*
kèwài 课外 *extra-curricular*
  kèwài huódòng 课外活动 *extra-curricular activity*
kòngr 空儿 *free time*
kùzi 裤子 *trousers, pants, slacks*
kuài 快 *quick*
  kuài...le 快······了 *soon...; nearly...*
kuài 块 *(MW for blackboard, rubber, watch)*
kùn 困 *sleepy*

L

lái 来 *come; (indicating intention to do something)*
Lánlán 兰兰 *(name)*
lán 蓝 *blue; (family name)*
  lán(sè) 蓝(色) *blue*
  Lán Lán 蓝蓝 *(name)*
  Lán Xīn 蓝新 *(name)*
lánqiú 篮球 *basketball*
Láojià..., 劳驾······ *Excuse me,...; Would you mind...?*
Láolā 劳拉 *Laura*
lǎo 老 *old*
  lǎoshī 老师 *teacher*
le 了 *(particle indicating that the action has been completed or, that a change has taken place)*
lèi 累 *tired; to be tired*
  lèisǐ 累死 *extremely tired*
lěng 冷 *cold*
Lǐ 李 *(family name)*
  Lǐ Fāng 李方 *(name)*
  Lǐ Míng 李明 *(name)*
  Lǐ Qiáng 李强 *(name)*
lǐmiàn 里面 *inside*
lǐtáng 礼堂 *hall, auditorium*
lìshǐ 历史 *history*
liǎ 俩 *two*
liǎn 脸 *face*
liàn 练 *to practise*
  liànxí 练习 *practise*
  liànxíběn 练习本 *exercise book*
liǎng 两 *two (of something)*
liàng 辆 *(MW for vehicles)*
Lín 林 *(family name)*
  Lín Fāng 林方 *(name)*
  Lín Hóng 林红 *(name*
  Lín Huá 林华 *(name)*
  Lín Lánlán 林兰兰 *(name)*
  Lín Qīng 林青 *(name)*
  Lín Yīng 林英 *(name)*
Líndá 琳达 *Linda*
líng 零(O) *nought*
Línglíng 玲玲 *(name)*
lǐngdài 领带 *necktie*

Liú 刘 *(family name)*
  Liú Xīnxīng 刘新星 *(name)*
liúlì 流利 *fluent*
liù 六 *six*
lóu 楼 *storeyed building; storey, floor*
  lóufáng 楼房 *storeyed building*
  lóushàng 楼上 *upstairs*
  lóuxià 楼下 *downstairs*
lù 路 *road*
lǜ(sè) 绿(色) *green*
luàn 乱 *in disorder, in a confusion; disorder, chaos*

M

māma 妈妈 *mother*
mǎ 马 *horse; (family name)*
  Mǎdīng 马丁 *Martin*
  Mǎkè 马克 *Mark*
  Mǎ Xiǎoqīng 马小青 *(name)*
Mǎlì 玛丽 *Mary*
ma 吗 *(question particle)*
mǎi 买 *to buy*
  mǎi dōngxi 买东西 *to shop*
màn 慢 *slow*
máng 忙 *busy*
māo 猫 *cat*
máo 毛 *hair; fur*
  máoyī 毛衣 *jumper (woollen)*
màozi 帽子 *hat, cap*
méi(yǒu) 没(有) *do not have; there is/are not; not*
  méi guānxi 没关系 *never mind*
  méi kòngr 没空儿 *not free; have no time*
  Méi shénme. 没什么。 *It's nothing.*
  méi yìsi 没意思 *uninteresting; boring*
měi 每 *every*
  měi tiān 每天 *every day*
měishù 美术 *art*
mèimei 妹妹 *younger sister*
mén 门 *(MW for school subjects); door*
  ménkǒu 门口 *entrance, doorway*
Mīmī 咪咪 *(name)*
míngbai 明白 *to understand*
míngnián 明年 *next year*
míngtiān 明天 *tomorrow*
míngzi 名字 *name*
mòjìng 墨镜 *sunglasses, dark glasses*

N

nà 那 *that; then; in that case*
  Nà hǎo,... 那好,…… *All right then,... (agreeing to a suggestion)*
  nàr 那儿 *there*
ná 拿 *take*
  náqu 拿去 *take away*
nǎli 哪里 *(polite response to praise)*
nǎr 哪儿 *where*
nán 南 *south*
nán 难 *difficult*
  nánkàn 难看 *ugly, unattractive*
  nán xué 难学 *difficult (of subjects for study)*

nán 男 *man, male*
  nán de 男的 *male; male person*
  nán cèsuǒ 男厕所 *male toilet*
  nán háir 男孩儿 *boy*
  nánshēng 男生 *male student*
  Nán Sì Zhōng 男四中 *(abbrev.) No. 4 Boys High School*
nǎojīn 脑筋 *brains; mind*
ne 呢 *(modal particle)*
něi 哪 *which*
nèi (also nà) 那 *that*
  nèige 那个 *that (one)*
  nèixiē 那些 *those (ones)*
néng 能 *can, be able to*
nǐ 你 *you (singular)*
  nǐ de 你的 *your, yours*
  nǐmen 你们 *you (plural)*
  nǐmen de 你们的 *your, yours (plural)*
  nǐ nàr 你那儿 *there (where you are); your place*
nián 年 *year*
  niánjí 年级 *year, grade, form*
niǎo 鸟 *bird*
nín 您 *you (polite)*
  Nín guì xìng? 您贵姓？ *(polite way of asking someone's family name)*
niúzǎikù 牛仔裤 *jeans*
nǚ 女 *woman, female*
  nǚ de 女的 *female; female person*
  nǚ cèsuǒ 女厕所 *female toilet*
  nǚ háizi 女孩子 *girl*
  nǚpéngyou 女朋友 *girlfriend*
  nǚshēng 女生 *female student*

O

Ó 哦 *(exclamation expressing doubt)*
Ò 哦 *(exclamation expressing understanding or realisation)*

P

pà 怕 *to fear*
  pà lěng 怕冷 *to dislike or feel the cold*
  pà rè 怕热 *to dislike or feel the heat*
páiqiú 排球 *volleyball*
pángbiān(r) 旁边(儿) *beside*
pàng 胖 *(of people) fat*
pǎo 跑 *to run*
  pǎobù 跑步 *to run*
pèi 配 *match*
  pèishàng 配上 *to match; match up*
péngyou 朋友 *friend*
pífū 皮肤 *skin*
píxié 皮鞋 *leather shoes*
pǐ 匹 *(MW for horse)*
piàoliang 漂亮 *attractive; beautiful*
pīngpāngqiú 乒乓球 *pingpong, table tennis*
Píngpíng 萍萍 *(name)*
pūtōng 扑通 *Plop! Splash!*

Q

qī 七 *seven*
qī 期 *period of time*
qí 骑 *to ride (astride)*
  qí chē 骑车 *to ride a bicycle*
  qí mǎ 骑马 *to ride a horse*
  qí zìxíngchē 骑自行车 *to ride a bicycle*
qíguài 奇怪 *strange, weird*
qǐ 起 *to rise*
  qǐchuáng 起床 *to get out of bed*
  qǐlai 起来 *(complement indicating an action*
    beginning and continuing)
qìchē 汽车 *car, bus, truck etc.*
qiān 千 *thousand*
qiānbǐ 铅笔 *pencil*
qiánmian 前面 *in front*
qiǎn 浅 *light, pale*
  qiǎn lánsè 浅蓝色 *light blue*
qīngwā 青蛙 *frog*
qǐng 请 *please; to invite*
  Qǐngwèn,... 请问,…… *Please may I ask...*
qiú 求 *to beg, request*
qiú 球 *ball*
  qiúchǎng 球场 *tennis court, football field etc.*
  qiúmí 球迷 *ball game enthusiast*
  qiúpāi 球拍 *racket, bat*
  qiúxié 球鞋 *gym shoes, sneakers*
qū 区 *region, district*
qù 去 *to go*
  qùnián 去年 *last year*
qúnzi 裙子 *skirt*

R

ránhòu 然后 *then; after that*
ràng 让 *let, allow; get someone to (do something)*
rè 热 *hot*
rén 人 *person; somebody*
rèn 认 *recognise; identify*
  rènshi 认识 *know (someone)*
róngyì 容易 *easy*
rúcǐ 如此 *like that*

S

Sàlì 萨莉 *Sally*
sān 三 *three*
  Sāntiáo 三条 *(place name)*
shǎo 少 *less, few*
shàng 上 *on; to attend (school); preceding; above*
  shàngbān 上班 *to go to work; to be at work*
  shàng gè xīngqī 上个星期 *last week*
  shàng gè yuè 上个月 *last month*
  shàngkè 上课 *attend class*
  shàngmian 上面 *on, above*
  shàngwǔ 上午 *morning*
  shàngxué 上学 *to go to school*
  shàngyī 上衣 *top (clothing)*
shéi 谁 *who*

shéi de 谁的 *whose*
shēn 深 *deep*
  shēn lánsè 深蓝色 *deep blue*
shēntǐ 身体 *body*
shénme 什么 *what*
shēng 声 *sound; voice*
shēngrì 生日 *birthday*
  shēngrìhuì 生日会 *birthday party*
shēngwù 生物 *Biology*
shīzi 狮子 *lion*
  shīzigǒu 狮子狗 *Shitzu (breed of dog)*
shí 十 *ten*
shíhou 时候 *time*
shíjiān 时间 *time*
shímáo 时髦 *fashionable*
Shǐmìsī 史密斯 *Smith*
shì 试 *to try; to test*
shì 是 *am, are, is*
  shìde 是的 *yes; right; that's it*
shì(r) 事(儿) *affair; matter*
shōushi 收拾 *to tidy up*
shǒu 手 *hand*
shòu 瘦 *thin*
shū 书 *book*
  shūbāo 书包 *schoolbag*
shūfu 舒服 *comfortable*
shùxué 数学 *Mathematics*
shuāng 双 *(MW) pair*
shuǐ 水 *water*
shuìjiào 睡觉 *to sleep*
shuìyī 睡衣 *pyjamas*
shuō 说 *to say; to speak*
  shuōhuà 说话 *speak, talk, say*
sì 四 *four*
...sǐ ……死 *(indicating an extreme) extremely*
suíbiàn 随便 *casual; random*
suì 岁 *years of age*

T

tā 它 *it*
tā 他 *he; him*
  tā de 他的 *his*
  tāmen 他们 *they; them*
    tāmen de 他们的 *their, theirs*
tā 她 *she; her*
  tā de 她的 *her, hers*
tài 太 *too*
  tài ... le 太……了 *extremely ...; too ...*
  tàitai 太太 *Mrs; wife*
táoqì 淘气 *naughty; mischievous*
tǎorénxián 讨人嫌 *annoy someone/people*
tǎoyàn 讨厌 *disagreeable; to dislike*
tào 套 *(MW) set*
tī 踢 *to kick; play (football)*
  tī zúqiú 踢足球 *play football*
tí 题 *examination questions; problem; topic*
tǐyù 体育 *physical education*
  tǐyù yùndòng 体育运动 *sports*
  tǐyù zhī jiā 体育之家 *family of sports enthusiasts*

tiān 天 day; sky; heaven
   tiānqì 天气 weather
   tiāntiān 天天 every day, daily
tiáo 条 (MW for fish, clothes)
tiào 跳 to jump; dance
   tiàowǔ 跳舞 to dance
   tiàoxia shuǐ 跳下水 jump into the water
tīng 听 to listen
   tīngdǒng 听懂 understand (through listening)
   tīngshuō 听说 to hear (about)
tíng 停 to stop
   tíngchē 停车 to park
tǐng ... de 挺……的 quite ...; very ...; rather ...
tóngbān 同班 same class; be in the same class
tóngxué 同学 fellow student
   tóngxuémen 同学们 fellow students
tóu 头 head
   tóufa 头发 hair
   tóu(r) 头（儿） top, end
túshūguǎn 图书馆 library
tuǐ 腿 leg
Tuōní 托尼 Tony, Toni

W

wàzi 袜子 socks, stockings
wàimian 外面 outside
wàitào 外套 coat, jacket
wàiyǔ 外语 foreign language
wán 完 finish; (complement of result)
wánr 玩儿 to play, enjoy oneself
wǎn 晚 late
   wǎnfàn 晚饭 evening meal
   wǎnshang 晚上 evening
Wáng 王 (surname)
   Wáng Bīn 王彬 (name)
   Wáng Bīng 王冰 (name)
   Wáng Lì 王力 (name)
   Wáng Xiǎomíng 王小明 (name)
   Wáng Xīng 王星 (name)
   Wáng Yàwén 王亚文 (name)
   Wáng Yǒng 王勇 (name)
wǎngqiú 网球 tennis
   wǎngqiúchǎng 网球场 tennis court
wàng 忘 forget
wèi 喂 hello; hey
wèi shénme 为什么 why
wèn 问 to ask
wǒ 我 I; me
   wǒ de 我的 my, mine
   wǒmen 我们 we; us
      wǒmen de 我们的 our, ours
      wǒmen zhèr 我们这儿 here (where we are); our place
   wǒ zhèr 我这儿 here (where I am)
wúliáo 无聊 bored
wǔ 五 five

wǔ 舞 dance
wǔfàn 午饭 lunch
wù 勿 (indicates prohibition)
wùlǐ 物理 Physics

X

xīyān 吸烟 to smoke
xīzhuāng 西装 suit
xǐhuan 喜欢 to like
xià 下 to fall (of rain, snow, hail); to leave; next
   xià (gè) xīngqī 下（个）星期 next week
   xià gè yuè 下个月 next month
   xiàkè 下课 to finish class
   xiàmian 下面 under, below
   xiàwǔ 下午 afternoon
   xià yì jié 下一节 next class
   xià yǔ 下雨 to rain
xiān 先 first; before; earlier
   xiānsheng 先生 Mr; gentleman
xiànzài 现在 now
xiǎng 想 intend, want to; think
   xiǎnghǎo 想好 to consider and come to a conclusion
xiǎo 小 small
   xiǎo gǒu 小狗 puppy
   xiǎoháir 小孩儿 child
   Xiǎo Hóng 小红 (name)
   Xiǎo Huá 小华 (name)
   xiǎojie 小姐 Miss; young lady
   xiǎomàibù 小卖部 tuckshop
   Xiǎo Míng 小明 (name)
   xiǎo shēng 小声 (of sound) softly
   xiǎoshí 小时 hour
   xiǎoshuō 小说 novel
   xiǎoxué 小学 primary school
   Xiǎo Yún 小云 (name)
   xiǎozǔ 小组 small group; group
xiào 笑 to laugh, smile
xiàofú 校服 school uniform
xiàohuì 校会 school assembly
xiàozhǎng 校长 school principal
xiē 些 several
xié 鞋 shoes
xiě 写 write
   xiě zì 写字 to write
xiè 谢 to thank; (family name)
   Xiè Hànshēng 谢汉生 (name)
   xièxie 谢谢 thank you
xīn 新 new
   xīncháo 新潮 trendy; latest fashion
   xīnshēng 新生 new student
xīngqī 星期 week
   xīngqī'èr 星期二 Tuesday
   xīngqīliù 星期六 Saturday
   xīngqīsān 星期三 Wednesday
   xīngqīsì 星期四 Thursday
   xīngqītiān 星期天 Sunday
   xīngqīwǔ 星期五 Friday
   xīngqīyī 星期一 Monday
xíng 行 be all right; OK
xìng 姓 surname; to be surnamed

xiūxi 休息 *to rest*
xǔ 许 *to allow; (family name)*
  Xǔ Yīng 许英 *(name)*
xué 学 *to study*
  xuéhuì 学会 *learn; master*
  xuésheng 学生 *student*
  xuéxiào 学校 *school*

Y

ya 呀 *(sentence particle)*
yán'gé 严格 *strict*
yánsè 颜色 *colour*
yǎnjìng 眼镜 *glasses*
yǎnjing 眼睛 *eye*
yáng 羊 *sheep; goat*
yǎng 养 *to keep, raise*
yàng 样 *appearance; shape; kind; type*
  yàngr 样儿 *appearance, shape*
  yàngzi 样子 *style; appearance*
yāo 幺 *one*
yáogǔnyuè 摇滚乐 *rock music*
yào 要 *want; intend; should, must, ought*
yě 也 *also*
yī 一 *one*
  yī céng 一层 *ground floor*
  yī lóu 一楼 *ground floor*
  yìbān 一般 *common, ordinary*
  yìdiǎnr 一点儿 *a little*
  yídìng 一定 *certainly, definitely*
  yígòng 一共 *altogether, in all*
  yíhuìr 一会儿 *a short while*
  yì jiā rén 一家人 *whole family*
  yìqǐ 一起 *together; in company*
  yì shēn(r) 一身(儿) *outfit, suit (of clothes)*
  yì tiān 一天 *a day*
  yíxià(r) 一下(儿) *(adds infomality to tone)*
yīfu 衣服 *clothes, clothing*
yǐhòu 以后 *after*
yǐqián 以前 *before*
yìsi 意思 *meaning*
yǐwéi 以为 *to think (mistakenly)*
yǐzi 椅子 *chair*
yīnyuè 音乐 *music*
  yīnyuèmí 音乐迷 *music enthusiast*
yīnggāi 应该 *should, ought*
Yīngwén 英文 *English language*
Yīngyǔ 英语 *English language*
yòng 用 *to use*
yóu 游 *to swim*
  yóuyǒng 游泳 *to swim*
  yóuxì 游戏 *game*
yǒu 有 *to have; there is, there are*
  yǒu kòngr 有空儿 *to be free; to have spare time*
  yǒu shíhou 有时候 *sometimes*
  yǒu shì(r) 有事(儿) *to be busy; to have something on*
  yǒu yìsi 有意思 *interesting*
  yǒu yòng 有用 *useful*

yòubian(r) 右边(儿) *on the right; right side*
yú 鱼 *fish*
yǔ 雨 *rain*
yǔwén 语文 *language and literature; Chinese (subject)*
yùxí 预习 *prepare lessons before class*
yuán 圆 *round*
yuánlái rúcǐ 原来如此 *So that's how it is.*
Yuēhàn 约汉 *John*
yuè 月 *month*
yùndòng 运动 *sport*
  yùndòngfú 运动服 *tracksuit*

Z

zázhì 杂志 *magazine*
zài 再 *again; once more*
  zàijiàn 再见 *goodbye*
zài 在 *at, in, on*
  zàijiā 在家 *be at home*
zánmen 咱们 *we; us (includes speaker)*
zǎo 早 *early*
  zǎofàn 早饭 *breakfast*
  zǎoshang 早上 *morning*
zěnme 怎么 *how*
  Zěnme la? 怎么啦? *What's the matter? Why?*
  zěnmeyàng 怎么样 *how*
  zěnyàng 怎样 *how*
zhāng 张 *(MW for table)*
Zhāng 张 *(family name)*
  Zhāng Yún 张云 *(name)*
zhǎng 长 *grow; develop; senior; head*
zháojí 着急 *to worry, feel anxious*
zhǎo 找 *to look for*
  zhǎo péngyou 找朋友 *to go to see friends*
zhè 这 *this*
  zhème... 这么...... *so...*
zhèi (*also* zhè) 这 *this*
  zhèige 这个 *this (one)*
  zhèi(gè) xīngqī 这(个)星期 *this week*
  zhèige yuè 这个月 *this month*
  zhèixiē 这些 *these (ones)*
  zhèiyàng 这样 *like this; this way; so; such*
  zhèr 这儿 *here*
zhēn 真 *really; true*
Zhēnnī 珍妮 *Jenny*
zhèng(zài) 正(在) *(aspect particle); in the process of*
zhèngzhì 政治 *politics*
zhī 之 *of (classical)*
zhī 支 *(MW for pencil, pen, etc.)*
zhī 只 *(MW for dog, cat, etc.)*
zhīdao 知道 *to know*
zhí 直 *straight*
zhǐ 只 *only; merely*
Zhōngguó 中国 *China*
  Zhōngguóhuà 中国话 *Chinese (language)*
  Zhōngguórén 中国人 *Chinese (person)*
zhōngjiān 中间 *centre, middle*

Zhōngwén　中文　*Chinese language*
zhōngwǔ　中午　*noon; midday*
zhōngxué　中学　*high school*
zhù　住　*to live*
zhù　祝……　*to wish (someone) ...*
zhuōzi　桌子　*table*
zǐ(sè)　紫（色）　*purple*
zì　字　*character; word; writing*
　　zìmǔ　字母　*(alphabet) letter*
zìjǐ　自己　*self*
zìxí　自习　*self-study session; study on one's own*
zìxíngchē　自行车　*bicycle*
zōng(sè)　棕（色）　*brown*
zǒu　走　*to walk; to leave*
　　zǒulù　走路　*to walk*
zúqiú　足球　*football*
zuì　最　*most*
　　zuì yòubian　最右边　*far right*
　　zuìhòu　最后　*last; final*
zuǐba　嘴巴　*mouth*
zuótiān　昨天　*yesterday*
zuǒbian(r)　左边（儿）　*on the left; left side*
zuò　坐　*to sit; to travel by*
　　zuò chē　坐车　*to travel by bus, car, train*
zuò　做　*to do*
　　zuòcuò　做错　*do wrongly*
　　zuò fàn　做饭　*do the cooking, prepare a meal*
　　zuò kèjiāncāo　做课间操　*to do set physical exercises*
　　zuòwán　做完　*to finish, complete*
　　zuò zuòyè　做作业　*to do homework*
zuòyè　作业　*homework*

Character list 汉字表

1. Characters are listed according to the number of strokes.
2. Characters with the same number of strokes are grouped according to their first stroke in the following order of stroke types:

   丶 *diǎn* 点   一 *héng* 横   丨 *shù* 竖   丿 *piě* 撇   ㄱ *gōu* 钩

   Characters within each group are listed in *pinyin* alphabetical order of stroke types.
3. References for characters that are appearing for the first time in Learn to Read and Learn to Write sections in *Hànyǔ for Intermediate Students, Stage 1* are listed in the right-hand columns. Characters that have appeared in these sections of *Hànyǔ for Beginning Students* are indicated with an asterisk.

				Learn to Write Lesson	Learn to Read Unit / Area
One stroke					
	一	yī *one*	星期一　一月　等一等	*	*
Two strokes					
【一】	二	èr *two*	星期二　二月	*	*
	七	qī *seven*	七月	*	*
	十	shí *ten*	十月	*	*
【丿】	八	bā *eight*	八月	*	*
	儿	er *(retroflex ending)*	有事儿　好玩儿	2	*
	几	jǐ *how many; several*	几个人？	*	*
	九	jiǔ *nine*	九月	*	*
	人	rén *person; people*	中国人　等人	*	*
【ㄱ】	了	le *(particle)*	养了　慢了　太好了	4	*
	力	lì *strength*	王力		3.4
Three strokes					
【丶】	门	mén *(measure word); door, gate*	两门课　出门　大门		4.4
	之	zhī *(auxiliary word)*	体育之家		1.5
【一】	才	cái *then (and only then)*	刚才		1.6
	大	dà *big*	很大　大学　澳大利亚	*	*
	干	gàn *to do*	干吗？　干什么？		1.4
	三	sān *three*	三月	*	*
	下	xià *leave; next, latter (as in xiàwǔ)*	下课　下个月 下个星期　下午　下一节课	*	*

【丨】	上	shàng	on top; attend; preceding, previous (as in zǎoshang)	上面		
			上课　上个星期　早上　上衣　穿上		*	*
	小	xiǎo	small	小学　小说　小点儿声	*	*
【丿】	个	gè	(measure word)	几个　两个　个子	*	*
	久	jiǔ	for a long time	好久不见了。	14	2.2
	么	me	(as in shénme)	什么　怎么	*	*
	千	qiān	thousand	一千	16	4.1
【ㄱ】	及	jí	to reach, attain	及格　不及格		4.7
	女	nǔ	woman; female	女的　女学生　女厕所	9	2.4
	习	xí	to practise; review	练习　复习	19	4.4
	也	yě	also		*	*
	子	zi	(noun suffix)	样子　裤子　名子	9	2.2

Four strokes

【、】	方	fāng	(as in Lín Fāng)	林方		*
	六	liù	six	六月	*	*
	认	rèn	to recognise; know	认识　学会认字	15	3.5
	为	wéi	to be, mean	以为		2.4
		wèi	for	为什么？	20	
	文	wén	script; writing; language	中文　语文	19	*
【一】	不	bù	not	不谢　不是　不热　不知道	*	*
	长	cháng	long	长裤　多长时间？	8	2.1
		zhǎng	grow; elder; senior	长高　校长	14	4.2
	车	chē	vehicle	自行车　汽车　公共汽车　坐车		*
	历	lì	to undergo	历史		4.4
	太	tài	extremely	太好了！　太大　太太	7	1.2
	天	tiān	day; heaven	今天　天气	*	*
	王	wáng	(a surname); king, prince		5	*
	五	wǔ	five	五月	*	*
	友	yǒu	friend	朋友　笔友		1.6

【丨】	见	jiàn	see	再见　一会儿见　看见　见到	12	*
	日	rì	day	生日　日本　星期日	*	*
	少	shǎo	few, less	多少？　穿得不少	7	*
	中	zhōng	middle	中国　中学　中午　初中　高中	*	*
【丿】	从	cóng	from	从八点到十点	21	
	分	fēn	minute; mark	十五分　三分钟　得多少分？	*	*
	公	gōng	public	公共汽车	11	1.2
	今	jīn	present	今天　今年	*	*
	气	qì	air	天气		*
	什	shén	(as in shénme)	什么？	*	*
	午	wǔ	noon, midday	上午　中午　下午	*	*
	月	yuè	month	一月　下个月	*	*
【┐】	办	bàn	to do, handle, manage	办公室　办公楼　怎么办？	11	3.1
	书	shū	book	看书　三本书　图书馆	12	*
	双	shuāng	(measure word) pair	这双黑鞋		2.3
	以	yǐ	according to	可以　以为	17	1.1

Five strokes

【丶】	白	bái	white	白衬衫　白色的	9	2.3
	半	bàn	half	十二点半　半个小时　半年	*	*
	边	biān	side	旁边　左边　右边		3.3
	汉	hàn	Han; Chinese	汉语　汉字		*
	记	jì	remember	记起来　记不起来　难记	19	3.4
	让	ràng	to let; allow	让他给我打电话。		1.6
	头	tóu	head	头发		2.4
	写	xiě	to write	写字　学会写字	16	
	主	zhǔ	main; primary	主任		4.2
【一】	本	běn	(measure word)	一本书　课本　日本	3	*
	打	dǎ	to strike; to play (ball games)	打球　打字　打电话	5	*

东	dōng	*east*	东西　买东西		2.2
功	gōng	*skill*	功课		4.5
节	jié	*(measure word)*	五节课　下一节（课）	17	4.2
可	kě	*can, may; (adverb used for emphasis)*	可以　可好看了。	18	*
去	qù	*to go; (as in qùnián)*	去打球　去年	2	*
右	yòu	*right*	右边		3.3
正	zhèng	*(aspect particle)*	正在　正好	4	*
左	zuǒ	*left*	左边		3.3
【丨】 北	běi	*north*	北京		*
出	chū	*out*	出去　出门		2.1
电	diàn	*electricity; electric*	电视　电话　电子	6	1.1
号	hào	*number; date*	几号？　五号房间	*	*
叫	jiào	*to be called*		*	*
旧	jiù	*old; used; worn*	旧课　旧衣服	20	4.5
四	sì	*four*	四月	*	*
史	shǐ	*history*	历史		4.4
兄	xiōng	*elder brother*	兄弟　兄弟姐妹		*
业	yè	*(as in zuòyè)*	作业	4	*
只	zhī	*(measure word)*	一只猫		*
	zhǐ	*only; merely*	只有		
【丿】 包	bāo	*bag; sack*	书包		3.4
乐	lè	*happy*	快乐		*
	yuè	*music*	音乐		3.2
们	men	*(pluralising suffix)*	我们　你们　他们	*	*
生	shēng	*to be born; (as in xuésheng)*	生日　学生　女生　男生	*	*
他	tā	*he, him*	他们	*	*
外	wài	*outside; foreign*	外面　外语　外国	12	
用	yòng	*to use*	借我用　很有用		1.3
【一】 对	duì	*right, correct; towards, to*	对了　对不起　对面	14	*
发	fà	*hair*	头发		2.4

Six strokes

【、】	关	guān	be concerned with	没关系。		4.7
	问	wèn	to ask	请问，……	11	*
	兴	xìng	desire to do something	高兴	15	3.5
	许	xǔ	to allow; permit	不许	18	4.3
	衣	yī	clothing	衣服　上衣　睡衣　游泳衣	7	2.1
	字	zì	character, word, letter	名字　汉字	*	*
【一】	百	bǎi	hundred	二百	16	4.1
	场	chǎng	place where people gather	球场	13	3.3
	地	dì	place; locality	地址	15	3.5
	动	dòng	to move	动物　运动		1.5
	共	gòng	altogether, in all; common	一共　公共汽车	17	1.2
	灰	huī	grey	灰色的	9	3.3
	考	kǎo	to give or take an examination	考试　考什么？ 考历史	22	4.7
	老	lǎo	old; (as in lǎoshī)	老师	*	*
	西	xī	west	东西		2.2
	亚	yà	(as in Àodàlìyà)	澳大利亚		*
	有	yǒu	to have	你有没有空儿？　教室里有人。	*	*
	再	zài	again	再见		*
	在	zài	at; on; (as in zhèngzài)	现在　正在　在家 在汽车前面	*	*
【丨】	吃	chī	to eat	吃午饭　吃得多	21	*
	刚	gāng	just; only a short while ago	刚才		1.6
	回	huí	to return; (measure word)	回家　回来　回去 怎么回事儿？	*	*
	吗	ma	(question particle)		*	*
	师	shī	teacher	老师	*	*
	岁	suì	years old, age	几岁？十二岁	*	*
	同	tóng	same; together with	同学们　同班	1	*
	早	zǎo	early	早上　早饭	*	*

【丿】	多	duō	*many; (indicating degree or extent)*	很多　多少？		
				多长时间？	4	*
	合	hé	*to suit*	合身		2.3
	后	hòu	*behind; back; rear*	后面　以后　然后	13	3.3
	会	huì	*to know how to; can; meeting; party; be likely to*			
				会做作业　一会儿　校会　生日会	16	1.4
	件	jiàn	*(measure word)*	三件衣服	8	2.3
	名	míng	*name*	名字	*	*
	年	nián	*year*	今年　明年　半年　哪年？	*	*
	任	rèn	*official post; office*	主任		4.2
	色	sè	*colour*	白色　蓝色的	13	3.3
	休	xiū	*to stop, cease*	休息		4.6
	行	xíng	*walk, travel, move; OK; be all right*	自行车　行吗？	3	*
	自	zì	*self; oneself*	自行车　自习		*
【コ】	好	hǎo	*good; well; (complement of result)*	你好！　挺好的		
				好听　好学　想好	*	*
	红	hóng	*red*	红裤子　红笔		2.3
	欢	huān	*joyfully*	喜欢　欢迎	1	1.1
	级	jí	*grade; level; rank*	九年级	17	4.2
	那	nà	*that*	那是……　那好，……　在那儿	*	*
		nèi	*that*	那个		
	妈	mā	*mother*	妈妈	*	*
	买	mǎi	*to buy*	买东西		2.2
	她	tā	*she, her*	她们	*	*

Seven strokes

【丶】	初	chū	*at the beginning of*	初中		4.2
	床	chuáng	*bed*	起床	*	*
	弟	dì	*younger brother*	弟弟　兄弟姐妹	*	*
	间	jiān	*within a definite time or space; room*	时间　中间　房间	11	3.1
	快	kuài	*happy; soon*	生日快乐！　快七岁了　跑得快		*

冷	lěng *cold*	怕冷　天气很冷		*	*
没	méi *not*	没有　还没(有)来　没什么		*	*
汽	qì *steam; vapour*	汽车			1.2
识	shí *to know*	认识		15	3.5
完	wán *to finish; complete*	做完练习　上完课		22	4.6
忘	wàng *to forget*	我忘了。　健忘			3.4
这	zhè *this*	这是……		*	*
	zhèi *this*	这个　这样			
【一】更	gèng *more; even more*	更快　更好		5	1.5
来	lái *to come*	来我家　一会儿回来　进来　看来		2	1.2
两	liǎng *two (of something)*	两个弟弟　两只猫			*
声	shēng *sound; voice*	小点儿声			4.3
找	zhǎo *to look for*	找朋友　找老师　好找		11	1.4
址	zhǐ *location; site*	地址		15	3.5
走	zǒu *to walk*	走路　走得慢　我走了。			*
还	hái *still, also; (as in* háishi)	还有　还是			
	huán *to return*	还书			1.1
进	jìn *to enter*	请进!　进来		14	*
运	yùn *motion; movement*	运动			1.5
【丨】吧	ba *(modal particle)*	走吧　他是学生吧?			1.2
别	bié *do not*	别忘了			4.5
步	bù *step*	跑步			1.5
吵	chǎo *quarrel; make a noise*	吵什么?　不要吵!			4.3
里	lǐ *in; inside*	里面　家里　家里人		18	3.4
男	nán *male person*	男生　男老师		9	3.3
时	shí *time*	时候　小时　时间		17	1.6
听	tīng *to listen*	听说　听懂		19	1.2
呀	ya *(particle)*	他呀,……　买东西呀?			2.2
【丿】饭	fàn *meal*	吃午饭		21	*
利	lì *(as in* Àodàlìyà); *sharp*	澳大利亚			*

每	měi every 每天		9	*
你	nǐ you (singular) 你们		*	*
身	shēn body 身体			2.3
体	tǐ body 体育			1.5
条	tiáo (measure word) 一条长裤		8	2.2
我	wǒ I; me 我们 我的		*	*
系	xì to be related to 没关系			4.7
迎	yíng to greet; welcome 欢迎			3.5
住	zhù to live 他住哪儿？		*	*
作	zuò to do, act, compose, write 作业		4	*
坐	zuò to sit; to travel by … 坐车 请坐。			*
【乛】层	céng storey; floor 二层			3.1
张	zhāng to stretch; open; (a surname) 不要紧张 张老师			4.7

Eight strokes

【丶】衬	chèn lining 衬衫			2.3
定	dìng to decide, fix, set 一定			4.7
房	fáng room; house 房间		11	3.1
放	fàng let go, release; put, place 放学		*	*
话	huà words; remark; language 电话 中国话 说话		6	1.6
京	jīng capital 北京			*
空	kòng spare time 有空儿			1.4
怕	pà to fear, be afraid of; dislike 怕冷 怕吵 怕考试			*
衫	shān unlined upper garment 衬衫			2.3
视	shì to look at 电视 视听室		14	1.1
试	shì try; test 试一试 试试看 考试		22	2.3
学	xué to learn 学汉语 上中学 难学		*	*
育	yù to educate; bring up 体育			1.5

【一】	表	biǎo	*watch; table*	汉字表		*
	厕	cè	*lavatory; toilet*	男厕所　女厕所		3.3
	到	dào	*arrive at; go to; resultative complement*			
				从三点到五点　到了　见到	21	4.6
	林	lín	*(a surname); forest*	林方		*
	拍	pāi	*bat; racket*	球拍		3.3
	事	shì	*affair, business*	有事儿　没事儿	2	*
	玩	wán	*to have fun; play*	好玩儿	2	2.4
	英	yīng	*(abbrev. of 英国 England)*	英语　英文	19	4.4
	现	xiàn	*now*	现在	*	*
【丨】	非	fēi	*not; no*	非常		1.1
	国	guó	*country*	中国　哪国人？		*
	明	míng	*bright, clear*	明天　明年　小明	*	*
	呢	ne	*(sentence particle)*	你呢？　球拍呢？	*	*
	图	tú	*picture; chart; map*	图书馆　地图		3.3
	些	xiē	*some, several; (measure word)*	这些……　那些……		3.3
	易	yì	*easy*	容易	22	1.4
【丿】	爸	bà	*father*	爸爸	*	*
	的	de	*(structural particle)*	朋友的　白色的　长一点儿的	*	*
	肥	féi	*fat; (of clothing) loose*	裤子太肥了		3.2
	服	fú	*clothes*	衣服	7	2.1
	狗	gǒu	*dog*	一只狗　狮子狗		*
	和	hé	*and, with*	弟弟和妹妹　和他一起去	*	*
	朋	péng	*friend*	朋友		1.6
	所	suǒ	*place*	厕所		3.3
	物	wù	*thing; matter*	生物　动物		4.5
	知	zhī	*to know*	知道	6	*
【乛】	姐	jiě	*elder sister*	姐姐　小姐	*	*
	练	liàn	*to practise; train*	练习	19	4.4
	妹	mèi	*younger sister*	妹妹　兄弟姐妹	*	*

Nine strokes

【丶】	穿	chuān *to wear*	穿衣服	7	2.1
	觉	jiào *sleep*	睡觉	*	*
		jué *to feel*	觉得		2.2
	亮	liàng *bright*	漂亮	13	2.4
	前	qián *front*	前面　以前	13	3.1
	室	shì *room*	办公室　教室	12	3.1
	说	shuō *to say*	说话　怎么说？　说汉语　小说		
			听说	3	*
	养	yǎng *to raise, keep, grow*	养狗　养猫		*
	音	yīn *sound*	音乐		3.2
	泳	yǒng *to swim*	游泳		1.5
	语	yǔ *language*	汉语　英语　语文		*
	祝	zhù *to express good wishes*	祝你生日快乐！		*
【一】	帮	bāng *to help*	帮我……　你可以帮我的忙吗？	20	*
	带	dài *to bring*	带汉语课本　我带你去		1.3
	面	miàn *face; side; aspect*	里面　外面　见面	12	3.1
	挺	tǐng *rather, quite; very*	挺好的	14	*
	要	yào *to want; have to; need to*	要哪个？　要多穿衣服		
			不要说话	7	*
【丨】	点	diǎn *o'clock*	三点半　一点儿	*	*
	哪	nǎ *which, what*	住哪儿？	*	*
		něi *which*	哪个？　哪国人？	*	*
	是	shì *is, are*	我是学生。是的	*	*
	星	xīng *star*	星期四　每个星期	*	*
	咱	zán *we (including the speaker)*	咱们		*
	昨	zuó *yesterday*	昨天		*
【丿】	复	fù *again*	复习	20	4.5
	很	hěn *very*	很好　很大	*	*
	看	kàn *to look, watch, read*	看书　好看　难看　看来	3	*

胖	pàng	fat; plump	挺胖的	10	2.4
狮	shī	lion	狮子狗		2.4
怎	zěn	how	怎么？ 怎么样？ 怎么办？	14	*
钟	zhōng	time measured in hours and minutes; clock	三点钟 分钟	21	4.6
【フ】给	gěi	to give	给你 借给 还给	21	*
孩	hái	child	孩子 女孩子 男孩子 小孩儿	10	2.4

Ten strokes

【丶】高	gāo	tall; high	个子很高 高中	10	2.4
家	jiā	home; family	我家 家里 在家	*	*
课	kè	lesson	课本 上课 下课 音乐课	13	*
旁	páng	side	旁边		3.5
请	qǐng	request, ask; please; invite	请进！	11	*
容	róng	to permit; allow	容易 容易学	22	1.4
谁	shéi	who	谁的 跟谁去？	*	*
息	xī	to stop, cease	休息		4.6
站	zhàn	station; stop; to stand	车站		3.4
【一】班	bān	class; shift	三班 同班 上班 班主任	17	4.2
都	dōu	all	他们都喜欢。	1	1.1
赶	gǎn	catch up with; rush through	赶作业		4.7
哥	gē	elder brother	哥哥	*	*
格	gé	standard	及格		4.7
配	pèi	to match	白衬衫配红裤子 配起来		2.3
起	qǐ	to rise, get up	起床 配起来 记不起来 和他一起	*	*
热	rè	hot	天气很热 怕热	*	*
校	xiào	school	学校 校长	*	*
样	yàng	appearance; shape	怎么样？ 样子 他长得什么样儿？	14	1.2
真	zhēn	real, true; genuine	真好玩儿 真的吗？	5	*
【丨】啊	a	(indicating questioning tone)	咱们去啊？		1.4

	紧	jǐn	*tight; taut*	紧张	这条裤子太紧了！		4.7
	哦	ò	*(exclamatory word)*	哦，我知道。			3.1
【丿】	笔	bǐ	*writing implement*	红笔	笔友		*
	候	hòu	*time; season*	时候		17	1.6
	健	jiàn	*to strengthen; healthy*	健身操	健忘		3.2
	借	jiè	*to borrow, lend*	借给他	跟他借	3	*
	拿	ná	*to take*	拿去吧！	我去拿		1.3
【乛】	难	nán	*unpleasant; difficult*	难看	难学	19	3.2
	能	néng	*can; be able to*	能跟我打球	我不能去。		1.4

Eleven strokes

	黄	huáng	*yellow*	黄衬衫	黄色的		2.3
【一】	教	jiào	*instruct, teach*	教室	教室楼	12	3.1
		jiāo	*teach, instruct*	他教汉语			4.6
	球	qiú	*ball*	打球	球场	5	*
【丨】	常	cháng	*often*	常去打球	常常	13	1.1
	啦	la	*(fusion of 了 and 啊)*	怎么啦？			1.3
	眼	yǎn	*eye*	眼睛	眼镜(儿)	10	2.4
【丿】	猜	cāi	*to guess*	猜一猜	猜猜看		3.2
	得	děi	*must; have to*	我得去			1.4
		de	*(structural particle)*	跑得很快		5	1.5
	第	dì	*(indicating ordinal number)*	第一节课	第二天	20	4.5
	馆	guǎn	*place for cultural activities*	图书馆			3.3
	猫	māo	*cat*	一只猫	养猫		*
	停	tíng	*to stop*	停车	停车场		4.3
	象	xiàng	*appearance; image*	好象			4.2
	做	zuò	*to do, make*	做作业	做完	4	*

Twelve strokes

【、】	道	dào	way; (measure word)	知道　六道题	6	*
	就	jiù	at once; right away; as soon as; right after; exactly; then; precisely; (ushers in a result) 有空就来看我。 就在前面。　下了课就还我。		19	1.6
	裤	kù	trousers	一条裤子　长裤	8	2.1
	裙	qún	skirt	裙子	9	2.4
	谢	xiè	to thank	谢谢　不谢　不用谢		*
	游	yóu	to swim	游泳　游得更快		1.5
【一】	期	qī	period of time	星期四　哪期的？	*	*
	喜	xǐ	to like; be fond of	喜欢	1	1.1
【丨】	黑	hēi	black	黑裤子　一双黑鞋		2.3
	跑	pǎo	to run	跑步　跑得快		1.5
	晚	wǎn	evening, night; late, to be late	晚上　晚了	*	*
	最	zuì	most	最大　最好　最喜欢　最后　最右边		1.1
【丿】	等	děng	to wait	等一等　等人		3.2
	短	duǎn	short	短裤　短文		2.2
	然	rán	so; like that	然后		4.6

Thirteen strokes

【、】	新	xīn	new	新课　新衣服	20	4.4
	数	shù	number	数学	19	4.4
【一】	蓝	lán	blue; (surname)	蓝(色)的　蓝裤子	9	
	楼	lóu	storeyed building	办公楼　教室楼　楼下　楼上	11	3.1
	想	xiǎng	to think; want	想看电影　想一想	18	1.2
【丨】	跟	gēn	(preposition) with; and	跟他借　跟谁去？	12	1.3
	睛	jīng	eye	眼睛	10	2.4
	路	lù	road, way	走路		*
	睡	shuì	to sleep	睡觉　睡衣	*	*
【丿】	错	cuò	wrong; mistake; (complement of result) 不错　做错 打错电话			4.6

Fourteen strokes

【、】	慢	màn	*slow*	表慢了　跑得慢　慢走。		*
	漂	piào	*(as in piàoliang)*	漂亮	13	2.4
	瘦	shòu	*thin; lean*	他太瘦了！　我瘦了		3.4
	髦	máo	*fashionable*	时髦　赶时髦		3.2

Fifteen strokes

【、】	澳	ào	*(as in Àodàlìyà)*	澳大利亚		*
	懂	dǒng	*to understand*	懂了　听懂		3.2
【一】	鞋	xié	*shoe*	黑鞋　球鞋		2.3
【丨】	影	yǐng	*shadow*	电影	8	1.2
	题	tí	*problem; topic*	考试题　六道题	22	4.7

Sixteen strokes

| 【一】 | 操 | cāo | *drill; exercise* | 健身操　做操　课间操 | | 3.2 |
| 【丿】 | 镜 | jìng | *lens; mirror* | 眼镜 | | 3.4 |

Seventeen strokes

| 【一】 | 戴 | dài | *to wear (hat, glasses, etc.)* | 戴眼镜 | | 3.4 |

Index to grammar and usage references

Vocabulary references

Classroom phrases

Instructions to students

On classroom procedure

上课！ Shàngkè! *Let's begin!*

下课！ Xiàkè! *Class dismissed!*

起立！ Qǐlì *Rise!* *(said by class monitor when teacher comes in and before the teacher leaves)*

坐下！ Zuòxià! *Be seated.*

站起来。 Zhàn qilai. *Stand up.*

到前面来。 Dào qiánmian lái. *Come to the front of the class.*

回到坐位上去。 Huídào zuòwèi shangqu. *Go back to your seat.*

请看黑板/写字板。 Qǐng kàn hēibǎn / xiězìbǎn. *Please look at the blackboard / board.*

打开课本/练习本。 Dǎkāi kèběn / liànxíběn. *Please open your (text) books / exercise books.*

请翻到第五页。 Qǐng fāndào dì 5 yè. *Please turn to page 5.*

请大家看第三行。 Qǐng dàjiā kàn dì 3 háng. *(Everyone) look at the 3rd line.*

看倒数第三行。 Kàn dàoshǔ dì 3 háng. *Look at the 3rd line from the bottom (of the page).*

再看第四段。 Zài kàn dì 4 duàn. *Let's go on and look at paragraph 4.*

把书合上。 Bǎ shū héshang. *Close your books.*

When practising

我念。 Wǒ niàn. *I'll read.*

你们听。 Nǐmen tīng. *You listen.*

跟我念。 Gēn wǒ niàn. *Read after me.*

马丁，你来念。 Mǎdīng, nǐ lái niàn. *Martin, you read it.*

你们轮流念。 Nǐmen lúnliú niàn. *(You) take turns reading it.*

一个一个来。 Yí gè yí gè lái. *(Do it) one by one.*

我问。 Wǒ wèn. *I'll ask questions.*

你们回答。 Nǐmen huídá. *You answer.*

你们先想两分钟。 Nǐmen xiān xiǎng liǎng fēnzhōng. *You have two minutes to think it over.*

先听录音，然后回答问题。 Xiān tīn lùyīn, ránhòu huídá wèntí. *You'll listen to the recording first, then answer some questions.*

一对儿一对儿地练习。 Yí duìr yí duìr de liànxí.   *Work in pairs.*

分成小组。 Fēnchéng xiǎozǔ.   *Divide into small groups.*

分成三组。 Fēnchéng sān zǔ.   *Divide into three groups.*

四个人一组。 Sì gè rén yì zǔ.   *Four to a group.*

编一个对话。 Biān yí gè duìhuà.   *Make up a dialogue.*

玛丽，你来汇报一下儿。 Mǎlì, nǐ lái huìbào yíxiàr.   *Mary, could you report (your findings) to the class.*

When cautioning students

注意听。 Zhùyì tīng.   *Listen carefully.*

注意发音。 Zhùyì fāyīn.   *Pay attention to your pronunciation.*

注意声调。 Zhùyì shēngdiào.   *Pay attention to your tones.*

When assigning homework

（我）现在布置作业。 (Wǒ) xiànzài bùzhì zuòyè.   *Here's your homework.*

下星期一交。 Xià xīngqīyī jiāo.   *It's to be handed in next Monday.*

写上姓名、班级。 Xiěshang xìngmíng, bānjí.   *Write down your name and class on it.*

When 'law and order' needs to be enforced!

坐好了！ Zuòhǎo le!   *Sit up straight!*

小点儿声！ Xiǎo diǎnr shēng!   *Be quiet!*

注意听讲！ Zhùyì tīng jiǎng!   *Pay attention!*

认真一点儿！ Rènzhēn yìdiǎnr!   *Be serious!*

别开玩笑！ Bié kāi wánxiào!   *Stop trying to be funny!*

不许说话！ Bùxǔ shuōhuà!   *Don't talk!*

下了课来找我！ Xiàle kè lái zhǎo wǒ!   *Come to see me after class!*

Requests to the teacher

报告！ Bàogào!   *Reporting! (said outside the door, when you are late)*

我可以记笔记吗？ Wǒ kěyǐ jì bǐjì ma?   *May I take notes?*

请您再说一遍。 Qǐng nín zài shuō yí biàn.   *Could you please repeat that?*

请您再放一遍。 Qǐng nín zài fàng yí biàn.   *Could you please play (the tape) once again?*

请你说得慢一点儿。 Qǐng nín shuō de màn yìdiǎnr.   *Could you please speak more slowly?*

我想不出来。 Wǒ xiǎng bù chulai.   *I can't think of the answer.*

我不懂/明白。 Wǒ bù dǒng/míngbai.   *I don't understand.*

我还不懂/明白。 Wǒ hái bù dǒngmíngbai.   *I still don't understand.*

Rules of pronunciation, spelling and writing

What are tones?

1. Chinese is a tonal language in which every syllable has its specific tone. A change of tone involves a change of meaning. For example:

   qìchē car 　　*qí chē* to ride a bicycle
   hǎo good 　　*hào* number
   dà big 　　*dǎ* to play (ball games)

2. In Standard Chinese (or *pǔtōnghuà*) there are four basic tones represented by tone marks. For example:

1st tone	2nd tone	3rd tone	4th tone
tā	*tóngxué*	*wǒ*	*zàijiàn*

3. When speaking there are also syllables that are unstressed and take a feeble tone. This is known as the neutral tone and is represented by a small circle above the vowel. Usually this tone mark is left out. For example:
   Nǐ ne̊? or *Nǐ ne?*

Position of tone marks

1. In the *pīnyīn* system of romanisation the tone mark is always placed over a vowel (e.g. *nǐ, wǒ, tā*).
2. If the syllable contains three vowels, the tone mark is placed over the middle vowel (e.g. *xiǎo*).
3. If the syllable contains two vowels, the tone mark is placed over the first vowel (e.g. *hǎo, zài*) unless the first vowel is an *i* or a *u*, in which case it is placed over the second vowel (e.g. *xiè, xué*).
4. When a tone mark is placed over an 'i', the dot over the 'i' is dropped.

Tone changes

Sometimes a tone is affected by other tones.

1. One example is the 3rd tone. When two or more 3rd tones immediately follow each other, only the *last* one is pronounced in the 3rd tone, the preceding ones are pronounced as 2nd tones. For example:

   Nǐ hǎo! is pronounced *Ní hǎo!*
   (Note that *Nǐmen hǎo* is still pronounced as *Nǐmen hǎo* because the suffix *-men* comes between the two 3rd tone syllables *nǐ* and *hǎo*.)

2. When a 3rd tone is followed by a 1st, 2nd or 4th tone or most neutral tones, it usually becomes a half-third tone, i.e. the tone only falls but does not rise. Note that when a 3rd tone is pronounced as a half-third tone its tone mark remains unchanged. For example:

   xiǎoshuō dǎ qiú kě'ài nǚ de

3. Another word that changes its tone is *bù*. When *bù* is followed by a 4th tone (or a neutral tone that was originally a 4th tone), it is pronounced in the 2nd tone. For example:

   bú shì
   bú tài gāo
   bú duì

4. The number *yī* is pronounced in the 1st tone when standing by itself. When it is followed by another syllable it changes its tone.

Yī followed by	changes into	example
4th tone or neutral tone	2nd tone	*yí liàng qìchē* *yí ge xuésheng*
all other tones	4th tone	*yì zhī māo* *yì píng niúnǎi* *yì běn shū*

Rules of phonetic spelling

1. When a syllable beginning with *a, o* or *e* follows another syllable in such a way that the division of the two syllables could be confused, an apostrophe is put in to mark the division clearly to avoid ambiguity. For example:

   kě'ài shí'èr

2. At the beginning of a syllable, *i* is written as *y*. For example:

   ia–ya ie–ye iao–yao iou–you ian–yan in–yin iang–yang ing–ying iong–yong

   I is written as *yi* when it forms a syllable by itself.

3. At the beginning of a syllable, *u* is written as *w*. For example:

   ua–wa · uo–wo uai–wai uei–wei uan–wan uen–wen uang–wang ueng–weng

   U is written as *wu* when it forms a syllable by itself.

4. At the beginning of a syllable, *ü* is written as *yu*. For example: *üe–yue üan–yuan ün–yun ü* is written as *yu* when it forms a syllable by itself.

5. When *ü* or the finals* that begin with *ü* appear after *j, q* or *x, ü* is written as *u,* with the umlaut omitted. For example:

   xué jù qǔ yú

Stress

Pǔtōnghuà, or Standard Chinese, distinguishes roughly three degrees of stress in polysyllablic words: main (or strong) stress, medium stress and weak stress.

1. In most disyllabic words, the strong stress falls on the second syllable, and the first syllable is usually pronounced with a medium stress. For example:

   Hànyǔ lǎoshī zàijiàn dǎ qiú qìchē diànshì

2. Most words of three syllables have the main stress falling on the last syllable. The usual stress pattern is 'medium-weak-strong'. For example:

   túshūguǎn Zhōngguórén zìxíngchē pīngpāngqiú

   * A Chinese syllable is usually made up of an initial (the beginning consonant) and a final (a vowel, a compound vowel or a vowel plus a nasal consonant). For example:

   mā hǎo běn m, h and b are the initials; a, ao and en are the finals.